WOMEN'S EMANCIPATION DURING THE PROPHET'S LIFETIME

MUSLIM WOMEN'S
ATTIRE AND ADORNMENT

Volume 4

Abd al-Halim Abu Shuqqah

Translated and Edited by
Adil Salahi

KUBE
PUBLISHING

Muslim Women's Attire and Adornment

First published in England by
Kube Publishing Ltd
Markfield Conference Centre,
Ratby Lane, Markfield,
Leicestershire, LE67 9SY,
United Kingdom
Tel: +44 (0) 1530 249230
Fax: +44 (0) 1530 249656
Email: info@ kubepublishing.com
Website: www.kubepublishing.com

WOMEN'S EMANCIPATION DURING THE PROPHET'S LIFETIME

CIP data for this book is available from the British Library.

ISBN: 978-1-84774-181-3 *Paperback*
ISBN: 978-1-84774-182-0 *Ebook*

Translate and Edit by: Adil Salahi
Cover Design by: Nasir Cadir
Typeset by: nqaddoura@hotmail.com
Printed by: Imak Offset, Turkey

Contents

CHAPTER 6: The veil, prior to Islam and after it

CHAPTER 7: Other Conditions of women's attire and adornment

Transliteration Table

Consonants. Arabic

initial, unexpressed, medial and final: ء ʾ

ا	a	د	d	ض	ḍ	ك	k
ب	b	ذ	dh	ط	ṭ	ل	l
ت	t	ر	r	ظ	ẓ	م	m
ث	th	ز	z	ع	ʿ	ن	n
ج	j	س	s	غ	gh	هـ	h
ح	ḥ	ش	sh	ف	f	و	w
خ	kh	ص	ṣ	ق	q	ي	y

Vowels, diphthongs, etc.

short:	ـَ a		ـِ i		ـُ u	
long:	ـَا ā		ـُو ū		ـِي ī	
diphthongs:			ـَوْ aw			
			ـَيْ ay			

CHAPTER I

Introductory Notes

Why we do not use '*hijab*' for this volume's title

The subject matter of this volume is the sort of clothing and ornamentation a Muslim woman may wear in front of men who are unrelated to her, whether this be at home or outside. It is common usage by writers in our own time, and indeed by people generally, to refer to the sort of female clothing that is acceptable to Islam as the hijab and to refer to a woman who uses such dress as *muḥajjabah*, meaning 'hijab-wearing woman'. It is commonly said that there is nothing wrong with using special or new terms, and this is true. However, we prefer to avoid using this new term for several reasons:

1. The new term is unrelated to the linguistic meaning of the Arabic word *ḥijāb*. According to the authoritative and voluminous Arabic dictionary *Lisān al-'Arab*, i.e. the Arabic Tongue, *ḥijāb* is derived from the root *ḥajaba* which means 'to cover, hide, conceal, shield'. Thus, *ḥijāb* refers to what is used to cover, hide, etc. Therefore, whatever is used as a screen between two things is a *ḥijāb*.

2. The new term is unrelated to the meaning of the word *ḥijāb* as used in the Qur'an. We find the word in verses such as: 'he kept saying: "My love of good things is part of my remembering my Lord!" until it disappeared from sight.' (38: 32) This refers to the sun as it had set. 'She kept herself in seclusion from them.' (19: 17) This occurs in Mary's story as she kept herself in seclusion from her people. 'When you ask the Prophet's wives for something, do so from behind a screen: this makes for greater purity for your hearts and theirs.' (33: 53) This refers to the Prophet's companions, and younger Muslims, when they needed to ask the Prophet's wives for something.

   These verses use the word *ḥijāb* as meaning something that separates two sides. It cannot mean clothing that a person may wear, whatever type and measure such clothing is like. Even if such clothing covers the woman fully, including her face, she will still see people around her, and people will be able to see the figure of the woman even if she is wearing black from head to foot. The last of the three verses above indicates 'from behind a screen', which refers to something like a curtain used at home, to separate the women's place from the men's place.

3. The new term is unrelated to the meaning of *ḥijāb* as this word is used in the hadiths. Here are a few examples:

   - 'Umar said: 'I said: "Messenger of God, good and bad people enter your homes. Perhaps you may wish to order the Mothers of the Believers to be screened." God then revealed the verse giving the screening order.' (Related by al-Bukhari)
   - Anas ibn Mālik narrated: 'I know the matter of the *ḥijāb* and when it was revealed better than all people. It was

first revealed on the day of the Prophet's wedding with Zaynab bint Jaḥsh. The morning after the wedding, the Prophet invited people and they had their dinner and left. A few of them, however, remained at the Prophet's home and stayed for a long time. The Prophet (peace be upon him) rose and left, and I left with him so that they might leave... He then returned and I returned with him, and we found that they had left. The Prophet dropped the curtain between him and myself, and the [command of the] *ḥijāb* was revealed.' (Related by al-Bukhari and Muslim)

- 'Ā'ishah narrated: 'My uncle through breastfeeding came over and sought permission to come in. I refused to let him enter until I had asked God's Messenger (peace be upon him)... This took place after we were commanded to remain behind the *ḥijāb*.' (Related by al-Bukhari and Muslim)
- Anas narrated: 'The Prophet stopped three days between Khaybar and Madinah so as to have his wedding with Ṣafiyyah bint Ḥuyay... Some Muslims said: "She is either one of the Mothers of the Believers, or she is one his right hand possesses [i.e. a slave]." Then they said: "If he screens her, she is a Mother of the Believers, but if he does not, she is one he possesses." When he was about to leave, he prepared her place behind him [on his mount] and put a screen between her and the people.' (Related by al-Bukhari and Muslim)

These are only a few of the many hadiths that mention the *ḥijāb*, indicating that it means a screen or curtain. For more texts, reference may be made to the second chapter in Volume Five of this abridged edition of the work. This is a chapter that shows that the term *ḥijāb* as used in the hadiths entered in the two *Ṣaḥīḥ* anthologies of al-Bukhari and Muslim applies only to the Prophet's wives.

This is as far as the term *ḥijāb* and its usage in the Qur'an and the Sunnah goes. As for the clothing, attire and adornment of Muslim women, which we have chosen as the title for this volume, references in the Qur'an are as follows:

- 'Children of Adam, We have sent down to you clothing to cover your nakedness, and garments pleasing to the eye; but the robe of God-fearingness is the finest of all.' (7: 26)
- 'Tell believing women... not to display their charms except what may ordinarily appear thereof. Let them draw their head-coverings over their bosoms.' (24: 31) The verse uses the word *jayb*, which is rendered here as 'bosom'. Its literal meaning is 'the top opening of a garment' which may reveal a part of one's chest.
- 'Prophet! Say to your wives, daughters and all believing women that they should draw over themselves some of their outer garments. This will be more conducive to their being recognized and not affronted. God is much-forgiving, ever-merciful.' (33: 59)
- 'Such elderly women as are past the prospect of marriage incur no sin if they lay aside their [outer] garments, provided they do not make a showy display of their charms. But it is better for them to be modest.' (24: 60) The Arabic term *qawā'id* used in this verse refers to a woman who is past the menopause and can no longer become pregnant. As such, she is unlikely to be sought in marriage.

Texts in the Sunnah that refer to clothing and adornment are also numerous, but they do not use the term *ḥijāb* at all. Here are a few:

- 'Muslim women used to attend the Fajr Prayer with God's Messenger (peace be upon him) covering their heads with their cloaks.' (Related by al-Bukhari)

- ‘They held their lower garments, and tore a piece of their lower end to cover their heads with.’ (Related by al-Bukhari)
- ‘Some suits with silk portions were brought to God’s Messenger (peace be upon him)... He gave one suit to ‘Alī ibn Abi Ṭālib and said to him: “Cut it into head coverings for your women.”’ (Related by Muslim)
- ‘Maymūnah [the Prophet’s wife] used to offer her prayer wearing a robe and a head covering, but without a lower garment.’ (Related by Mālik in *al-Muwaṭṭa’*)
- Mālik said: ‘The best I heard concerning a person atoning for a broken oath by giving garments is that if he gives men, he should give them one robe each, and if he gives women, he should give them two each: a robe and a head covering. This is the least that either may wear when praying.’
- ‘A woman who is in a state of consecration, i.e. *ihrām*, may not wear a veil or gloves.’ (Related by al-Bukhari)
- When Subay‘ah al-Aslamiyyah finished her postnatal discharge and cleansed herself, she adorned herself for prospective proposals. (In a version related by Ahmad: she wore kohl and used reddish makeup.) Abu al-Sanābil entered her place...’ (Related by al-Bukhari and Muslim)

So far we have highlighted the different meanings of the terms *ḥijāb* and *libās*, which means clothing or attire. This distinction leads to different practical results which are intended and should be observed. The *ḥijāb*, as used in the Qur’an and the hadith, ensures that men do not see women and at the same time the women do not see men. Hence, when God commanded the Prophet’s wives to be screened, i.e. behind a *ḥijāb*, He added: ‘This makes for greater purity for your hearts and theirs’. (33: 53) The greater purity that men obtain is due to the fact that they would not see the Mothers of the Believers, while the greater purity the Prophet’s wives obtain is because they do not see men. On the other hand, whatever clothing a woman may wear, even if it covers her face, allows her to see men.

The *ḥijāb* applied to the Prophet's wives only, and not to any other women believers. This is clear when we bear in mind the linguistic meaning of this word, as we have explained. On the other hand, there is nothing special about clothing and attire. Everyone may wear these. The Prophet's wives used to observe the normal Islamic dress code when they went out. In this case, it is and was not called *ḥijāb*. Therefore, the *ḥijāb* refers to a particular aspect of manners which applied to the Prophet's wives only when they were at home. In this, they were a group apart from the rest of Muslim women, and this distinction is made in honour of God's Messenger (peace be upon him). This complements another aspect of manners that applied to the Prophet's wives, which is stated in another Qur'anic verse: 'And stay quietly in your homes.' (33: 33) Both aspects of manners are meant as a special status applicable to the Prophet's wives, in preparation to a further requirement that prevented them from marrying anyone after the Prophet had passed away. This comes at the end of the verse imposing the duty of screening on them: 'When you ask the Prophet's wives for something, do so from behind a screen: this makes for greater purity for your hearts and theirs. Moreover, it does not behove you to give offence to God's Messenger, just as it would not behove you ever to marry his widows after he has passed away. That is certainly an enormity in God's sight.' (33: 53)

We will discuss in the next volume of this work the evidence showing that the *ḥijāb* applied only to the Prophet's wives. This will show the extent of the error made by many people due to their overlooking how very special this requirement was. It makes it necessary, therefore, for us to distinguish between what was required of the Prophet's wives in particular and what is required of Muslim women generally.

The objectives of the Islamic dress code for women

The Islamic dress code for women fulfils two basic objectives. The first is covering the *'awrah,* i.e. the part of the body that must not be exposed, and preventing temptation. The second is that it is a kind of honour and distinction. We will discuss and explain both objectives.

Some contemporary people raise the question: If the first objective is covering the *'awrah*, why is it different for men and women when the physical appearance may be appealing and tempting in either direction? The answer is found in consideration of several points:

- The degree of temptation differs in the two cases. God has given the woman's body features that distinguish it from that of the man. Indeed, every part of the woman's body has its special appeal. A woman looks at a man's body as a whole and she does not concern herself with its details. This means that different parts of the man's body do not have a particular appeal to the woman. If this happens in some cases, it is of a mild degree. By contrast, each part of the woman's body has its own beauty and attraction. Indeed the practical behaviour of people gives us more than this. A man normally takes care of his appearance by wearing more clothes, covering more of his body so as to leave only his head and hands visible. By contrast, a woman shows her beauty by exposing more and more of her body. Perhaps this is due to the fact that a man's body is bigger and rougher while a woman's body is more refined and attractive.
- Their different fields of work. We are here speaking of the basic and essential work each of them does. The man is the family's breadwinner and he normally works outside the home. Most of the time, he does different types of work, which

makes it difficult for him to cover himself. The woman's work is mostly at home and with her children. As such, she does not need to cover all her body. When a woman works away from home for some personal or community need, this is a special case and she needs to tolerate the difficulty of covering herself. However, when the difficulty is burdensome or when a woman has to go out to work most of the time and she feels it hard to cover herself all the time, qualified scholars have to consider the extent of relaxation that may apply to her. There are certain rules that may apply in this case, such as 'hardship is a cause for relaxation', and 'needs are treated as necessities in permitting what is prohibited'. For example, would scholars reduce the head covering so that it covers a woman's hair but not her neck, when there is need to frequently move about and the weather is hot? Would they allow a woman to reveal a part of her arm when this is necessary for her work? The same may be asked about revealing a part of her leg when crossing a waterway? Consideration of this may take into account what some Ḥanafī scholars call 'exposure as a test'. 'Alī al-Marghīnānī, the author of *al-Hidāyah* and a distinguished Ḥanafī scholar, said: 'The entire body of a free woman is *'awrah*, apart from her face and hands. This is based on the Prophet's hadith: "The woman is a covered *'awrah*." Those two parts are excepted as their exposure serves as a test.'

> We may also refer to what happened at the time of the Battle of Uḥud, when the urgency of the task caused 'Ā'ishah and Umm Sulaym to lift their garments so as to reveal the lower part of their legs, as they rushed with waterskins, almost running, to give the wounded Muslim soldiers a drink.

- Although a man's *'awrah* is limited to a small part of his body, still human tradition, let alone the Islamic one, recommends men to cover a greater part of their bodies in all situations, so as to appear decent. This means that to only cover the *'awrah* is acceptable only when needed, which means in special situations. This particular situation of covering the *'awrah* only rarely happens. We should also bear in mind that generally speaking, a man's physical appearance is not particularly tempting for a woman.

The other objective, namely, honouring free Muslim women by distinguishing them from slaves is an appropriate purpose which is not based on worldly status, wealth or power.[1] It is an attitude that stresses a woman's honourable status, one who is chaste and virtuous. This requires a high standard of moral behaviour from the woman who is so attired and a response by other people that commands full respect and appreciation.

Appearance and essence

Discussion of clothing and attire leads us to talk about appearance and substance. In form and colour, clothes are the way a person appears, but in essence, they reflect something more. When a man or a woman selects their clothes, they have in mind three considerations: 1) covering the body; 2) suitability for weather conditions; and 3) to have a good appearance. This applies to clothing in general situations. However, in the case of the Muslim woman, it also has an overall consideration, which is fearing God: 'The robe of God-fearingness is the finest of all.' (7: 26) To it is added the hue of decency and chastity:

1. Muslim women slaves were not required to dress in the same way as free women, because of the tasks they were required to do, in the home and outside. The distinction in their appearance ensured that they were treated with respect in Muslim society. We praise God that slavery is ended and the discussion of how slave women should dress is only of academic, not practical, interest.

'This message takes its hue from God; who can give a better hue than God?' (2: 138) This is the essence of the Muslim woman's dress code. Valuable as it is, it is merely a small part of a greater essence. Wearing clothes is merely a small action, but it is a part of the greater essence of the Muslim woman's personality, intellect, emotion, dignity and responsibility. In order that the woman's personality be consistent, every part must be in line with the total. Thus:

- Full attire not only fulfils the requirements of decency and chastity, but also helps to enrich the woman's intellect so as to be more creative and innovative;
- Full attire helps to keep the woman's heart on the right track, so as to remain alert and full of goodness;
- Full attire helps the woman to maintain her dignity wherever she happens to be, and
- Full attire helps the woman to discharge her responsibilities, starting with taking care of her family home and including her contribution to the advancement of her community whether by social and political activity or by undertaking professional work to meet her own needs or the needs of her community.

Thus, a woman's personality remains consistent and life around her is set on the right basis.

When full attire becomes a reason to impose confinement within the home in all situations, or a hindrance preventing a woman from taking part in all spheres of life, including what is good and beneficial, it becomes a cause that stops her intellect, spreads darkness over her heart and detracts from her dignity. Ultimately, it undermines her responsibilities. Yet the woman is a human being God has created so that she can share with man the task of building life on earth in the purest and most perfect shape and form. God's Messenger (peace be upon him) says the truth: 'Women are men's full sisters.'

Any requirements of style or colour?

Islamic law does not make any requirement of style concerning women's attire, but it has certain conditions that should be observed in any style people accept. These differ from one community or country to another. Normally, Islam approves of social traditions unless a tradition is contrary to its rulings or values. In this respect, it did not alter the traditions of pre-Islamic society in respect of clothing; it only introduced certain necessary amendments.

Prior to Islam, Arabian women used to wear clothing of a certain style. These included the head covering, a robe which covers a person's body, a cloak which is worn over the head covering and the robe, and the veil or *niqab* which some women wear to cover their faces keeping only their eyes uncovered.

Islam introduced certain values applicable to such garments, urging women to observe them when they wear such clothes so that they fully cover their bodies. For example, when a woman wears a head covering, i.e. *khimār*, she should bring it low in front so that it covers her neck and the top opening of her robe. God says: 'Let them draw their head-coverings over their bosoms.' (24: 31) Islam also urges free women to wear a cloak or a cape when they go out so that they are distinguished as free women: 'Prophet! Say to your wives, daughters and all believing women that they should draw over themselves some of their outer garments. This will be more conducive to their being recognized and not affronted'. (33: 59)

Islam also requires women who are used to wearing the veil to take it off at certain times, such as when they pray. Prostration, which is an essential part of prayer, cannot be complete as manifestation of submission to God unless one's forehead and nose are placed on the floor. Also, the veil may not be worn during the time of consecration, or *iḥrām*. This is to put off whatever is an aspect of comfort in preference to aspects of showing humility before God. In an analogy with *iḥrām* some Ḥanbalī scholars do not permit wearing the veil when a woman is in mourning. They consider it an aspect of adornment.

These are some of the recommendations that are considered conditions to be fulfilled in whatever a woman wears when she meets men who are unrelated to her. We shall speak about the conditions in detail presently, but we would like to stress here that what is important is the substance, not the appearance. This means that primary consideration should be given to dress that covers adornment that may stir desire and cause temptation. It is to this that the Qur'an refers when it makes this requirement of Muslim women: 'Tell believing women... not to display their charms except what may ordinarily appear thereof.' (24: 31)

Styles of dress are not absolute matters of worship, but are related to the field of 'transactions' which are judged according to considerations of cause and the objectives of Islamic law. Moreover, they belong to matters of habit and tradition, which differ in different times and places. Any style of dress that meets the criteria of covering and is suited to the local climate, while enabling the wearer to move easily is acceptable from the Islamic point of view.

Here is a quotation from Imam Ibn Taymiyyah which throws further light on the fact that there is no harm in having multiple styles and colours of clothes, as long as these fulfil the conditions and values stated by the Legislator:

> When the Prophet's companions moved into other areas and provinces, every one of them used to eat of the local food and wear local dress. They did not seek the type of food and dress they used in Madinah. Had this been better from the Islamic point of view, they would not have hesitated to do it... In this light, the most common practice of the Prophet and his companions was that they wore their traditional

upper and lower garments. Does this mean that it is better for everyone to do the same, even when also wearing a shirt? Or is it better to wear a shirt and trousers, without the need for an old style upper and lower garments? This is also something on which scholars have differed, but the second viewpoint appears to be more correct.

Conditions of the women's Islamic dress code (when meeting unrelated men)

Two main conditions must be fulfilled with regard to the attire and adornment of a Muslim woman when she meets men who are unrelated to her. The first condition, which is concerned with women's dress, includes the five requirements listed below, while the second condition is concerned with her adornment. The five requirements are:

1. Covering the woman's entire body with the exception of her face, hands and feet;
2. Moderation in the adornment worn on a woman's clothes, face, hands and feet;
3. That the dress and adornment are acceptable to the Muslim community;
4. That the woman's attire is overall different from men's clothing and,
5. That the attire is overall different from what is distinctive of unbelieving women.

We shall devote the next five chapters (Chapters 2-6) to the evidence supporting what is required to meet the first condition, whether these are from the Qur'an or the hadiths. We will also discuss the controversy regarding the permissibility of showing women's faces, hands and feet.

CHAPTER II

The First Condition of Women's Clothing

Features of Women's Dress Code in the Qur'an

The features of a woman's Islamic dress code are included in two surahs of the Qur'an: Surah 33, The Confederates, which was revealed after the Encounter of the Moat, and Surah 24, Light, which was revealed after the Battle with the al-Muṣṭalaq tribe. There are different reports about the time of that battle, but most probably it took place around the middle of year 5 AH, while the Encounter of the Moat, which is also known as al-Khandaq Expedition, took place towards the end of the same year.

Feature 1: The ḥijāb *applies to the Prophet's wives only*

God says: 'Believers! Do not enter the Prophet's homes, unless you are given leave, for a meal without waiting for its proper time. But when you are invited, enter; and when you have eaten, disperse without lingering for the sake of mere talk. Such behaviour might give offence to the Prophet, and yet he might feel too shy to bid you go. God does not shy of stating what is right. When you ask the Prophet's wives for something, do so from behind a screen: this makes for greater purity for your hearts and theirs. Moreover, it does not behove you to give offence to God's Messenger, just as it would not behove you ever to marry his widows after he has passed away. That is certainly an enormity in God's sight.' (33: 53)

The verse says: 'When you ask the Prophet's wives for something, do so from behind a screen.' This is the sentence in which the word *ḥijāb* is used, and this word is rendered in translation as 'a screen'. It refers to a screen and a woman who is behind it. This means that when men talked to the Prophet's wives, a screen had to separate them so that the men did not see the Prophet's wives. The Prophet's wives were permitted to go out to attend to their personal needs. When they did so, they were required to cover their faces, along with the rest of their bodies. Thus, the *ḥijāb* has two forms: at home where the Prophet's wives talked to men from behind a screen and outside which required them to cover their faces.

In Volume 5 of this abridged series we devote Chapter 2 to a discussion of the *ḥijāb* mentioned in this verse and the proof that it applied only to the Prophet's wives.

Feature 2: Distinction between free and slave women

God says: 'Prophet! Say to your wives, daughters and all believing women that they should draw over themselves some of their outer garments. This will be more conducive to their being recognized and not affronted. God is much-forgiving, ever-merciful.' (33: 59) We will quote some of what books of commentary on the Qur'an have to say about this verse.

1. 'Commentators differ with regard to what is exactly meant by "draw over themselves". Some of them said that it means that they must cover their faces and heads, leaving only one

eye uncovered. Others said that this order means that they tie their outer garments over their foreheads.' (From *Jāmi' al-Bayān* by Muhammad ibn Jarīr al-Ṭabarī, died 310 AH, 922 CE)

Al-Ṭabarī quotes three reports in support of the first view: one by Ibn 'Abbās and the other two by 'Abīdah. He also quotes four reports supporting the second view: one by Ibn 'Abbās, one by Qatādah, a third by Mujāhid and the fourth by Abu Ṣāliḥ. However, the last two reports do not mention 'tying over their foreheads' but say that women should wear an 'outer garment' and 'cover their heads' with it.

2. 'Draw over themselves some of their outer garments' means that they let their garments and cloaks drop low so as to cover their main bodies. Thus, they are recognized as free women.' (From *al-Wajīz fī Tafsīr al-Qur'an al-'Azīz* by al-Wāḥidī, died 468 AH 1076 CE)
3. 'Al-Kisā'ī said that "draw over themselves" means that they cover their heads with their cloaks with which they wrap themselves. He explains drawing over as meaning wrapping themselves.' (From *al-Baḥr al-Muḥīṭ* by Abu Ḥayyān, died 754 AH, 1343 CE)

We gather from what Qur'anic commentators say that 'drawing over themselves' may take several forms:

1. Bringing it over the face, leaving only one eye uncovered. This is according to some reports mentioned by al-Ṭabarī and others.
2. Bringing it to one's forehead. This is according to some reports mentioned by al-Ṭabarī.
3. Bringing it down to one's face leaving the two eyes uncovered. This is according to a report by Ibn 'Aṭiyyah.
4. Letting down their top garments and cloaks. This is according to al-Wāḥidī. The same is said by Ibn Qutaybah as quoted

by Ibn al-Jawzī. Similarly, wearing a cloak or having some of what they have as an outer garment. This is one report by al-Ṭabarī quoting Mujāhid and one of two views expressed by al-Zamakhsharī.
5. Covering their heads with their cloaks with which they wrap themselves. This is mentioned by Abu Ḥayyān quoting al-Kisā'ī.
6. If the cloak refers to a robe, then drawing it over oneself means making it long so as to cover the body and legs. This is mentioned by al-Khaṭīb al-Shirbīnī quoting al-Khalīl.

All these forms are possible, but the most difficult of them all is that which requires a woman to hold the end of her cloak and draw it over her face, leaving one eye, or both eyes uncovered. This requires that one of her two hands will always remain holding her cloak, unable to help in any work that requires both hands, such as washing clothes or cultivating the land, as women do in rural areas, or collecting the dates, as mentioned in a hadith. Nor can she carry a child or a shopping bag, or examine something she wants to buy, or ride a mount and hold its rein. Moreover, God's Messenger (peace be upon him) ordered women to wear their cloaks when they aimed to attend the Eid Prayer. He said: 'Let her sister lend her one of her cloaks.' Furthermore, she needs to keep her hands free during prayer, so that she can perform some of the actions of prayer, such as lifting her arms when starting a movement and when bowing and prostrating. It may not be argued here that the woman's face is not part of the *'awrah* during prayer. On the contrary, as the Eid Prayer is offered in an open space, a woman attending the prayer is seen by men. Those who demand that women cover their faces claim that in such a case, covering her face is a duty of every woman. All this means that drawing her cloak over herself cannot always be coupled with covering her face.

A more relevant point is that if the Muslim woman is required to cover her face, this is better done by wearing a veil, or *niqab*, as it has several advantages: (1) it has always been known and understood; (2) it gives a stable cover; and (3) it is easier for the woman as it does not require her to be always holding her cloak to cover her face with.

We consider that the reports that speak of covering the woman's face leaving one eye uncovered speak of one acceptable form of 'drawing over themselves', not the only form that must be done. I think this is acceptable because it does not negate the acceptability of the other forms. Moreover, this form is particularly difficult. It may be considered in some cases, but not as the permanent case. If the reports are understood to mean that this is an obligatory form, then this is a wrong understanding. The claim that it is obligatory is countered by the Prophet's instruction: 'A woman in a state of consecration, i.e. *iḥrām*, may not wear a *niqab*.' This instruction means that wearing a *niqab* is permissible in situations other than that of consecration. Further, the *niqab* leaves both eyes uncovered, not just one. When we say that the form of uncovering one eye is one of a number of acceptable forms, we have the advantage of reconciling the different pieces of evidence, and do not set one text against another. We also have a good understanding of the relevant verses. Thus, the verse that says: 'they should draw over themselves some of their outer garments' (33: 59) refers to the need that free women distinguish themselves from slaves by this action. On the other hand, the other verse says: 'Tell believing women... not to display their charms except what may ordinarily appear thereof.' (24: 31) This allows leaving a woman's face and hands uncovered as they, and the adornment on them, are part of the apparent adornment that may be shown.

Our view allows us to reconcile the reports and views commentators have stated concerning the verse that requires Muslim women to 'draw over themselves some of their outer garments'. When we carefully consider the different forms suggested, we find that the second, fourth, fifth and sixth forms suggest drawing the woman's cloak or outer garment over her body generally, mentioning nothing about her face.

Some people try to prove that it is obligatory for a woman to cover her face citing these reports mentioned by al-Ṭabarī and other scholars. In response we say that these reports do not aspire to the status of valid religious evidence; they are merely indications a researcher may bear in mind. They may have some question marks about their authenticity, but regardless of this, they do not mention any verbal Sunnah, i.e. a hadith stated by the Prophet or a practical one he might have approved. They are no more than a preference stated by a scholar with regard to the meaning of 'draw over oneself', giving his own view of the covering a woman should maintain, at the time when such a scholar expresses his own reasoning. If, for argument's sake, we consider that these reports mention the action of some women during the Prophet's lifetime, i.e. stating a Sunnah by approval, this does not mean more than such action is permissible. It bears no evidence whatsoever suggesting an obligation. Anyway, different views have been expressed, and none is more valid than the others. No religious obligation can be determined on the basis of such differences.

We feel that the verse, 'they should draw over themselves some of their outer garments' (33: 59) is better understood in the light of the meaning mentioned by al-Zamakhsharī who highlights the usage of the word 'some' in the verse. He says that it means to wear 'some of what they have of outer garments'. This is close to Mujāhid's view quoted by al-Ṭabarī: 'They wear a cloak to show that they are free women.' The same applies to the above-mentioned forms, stated by Abu Ṣāliḥ and Ibn Qutaybah and reported by al-Ṭabarī. Further, it is close to what al-Khalīl says: 'If the cloak refers to a robe, then drawing it over oneself means making it long so as to cover the body and legs.'

Moreover, this view is close to what is mentioned in different hadiths. Subay'ah al-Aslamiyyah said: 'In the evening, I put on my clothes and went to see God's Messenger (peace be upon him).' Fāṭimah bint Qays said: 'I wore my clothes and went to see God's Messenger (peace be upon him).' Further, this view spares us the problem of trying to give the expression, 'draw over oneself,' a particular form to the exclusion of others. It admits all varied forms, each of which is reported in different ways in books of Qur'anic commentary. All of them can take place, albeit at different times.

We finally say to those who negate the permissibility of uncovering women's faces: if all these descriptions of the cloak or outer garment are possible, and all these forms of 'drawing over oneself' are possible, and they are all stated by highly eminent scholars, why should we choose one form and claim that it is obligatory, without clear evidence from the Qur'an, the hadith or an authentic statement by an honourable companion of the Prophet?

The report that 'drawing over oneself' means covering the face leaving only one eye uncovered is considered 'lacking in authenticity' when it is attributed to Ibn 'Abbās, who was a companion of the Prophet, but considered 'authentic' when attributed to 'Abīdah al-Salamānī who belonged to the *tābi'īn* generation. Does such authenticity make it more valid than authentic reports al-Bayhaqī attributes to Ibn 'Abbās, Ibn 'Umar and 'Ā'ishah, all of whom were learned companions of the Prophet? They all confirm that the reference in verse 24: 31 to women's 'charms that ordinarily appear' in front of men means their faces and hands.

Shaykh 'Abd al-Ḥamīd ibn Bādīs discusses the question in a scholarly way. He said:

> The Qur'anic verse implies that a Muslim woman should cover herself with her cloak and wrap herself with it, bringing it towards her face. This admits its applicability to all or a part of her face. The fact that the early commentators

differed concerning the exact meaning of the Qur'anic statement is in itself evidence of the validity of both possibilities... The best that has been quoted from leading Arabic linguists in explaining this verse is al-Kisā'ī's statement that Muslim women should 'cover their heads with their cloaks with which they wrap themselves.' Al-Zamakhsharī suggests that al-Kisā'ī 'explains drawing over as meaning wrapping themselves.' Needless to say, head covering does not necessarily mean covering the face fully.

Scholars expressed two views about this verse and both are quoted by Ibn Jarīr al-Ṭabarī in his famous commentary. The first suggests that it means that women should cover their faces and heads leaving only one eye uncovered. This is stated by 'Abīdah and Ibn 'Abbās through Abu Ṣāliḥ. The other is that women should wrap their cloaks over their foreheads. This is the view of Qatādah and also Ibn 'Abbās through Muhammad ibn Sa'd.

The first verse (24: 31) indicates that it is permissible to leave the woman's face and hands uncovered, as explained earlier. The second verse (33: 59) requires women to 'draw over themselves some of their outer garments.' This may mean that a woman should cover all her face, as the first view suggests, which means that it is in conflict with the first verse. It may also mean holding the woman's outer garment and bringing a part of it over her forehead, as the second view suggests. In this case, there is no conflict between the two verses. That Qur'anic verses should be understood as having no conflict is better and weightier, if not a duty.

Furthermore, the second verse mentions the purpose of what is required of Muslim women: 'They should draw over

> themselves some of their outer garments. This will be more conducive to their being recognized and not affronted.' (33: 59) The reason, then, is that free women are distinguished from slaves who used to go out without a head covering or a partial one. They were affronted by evil people. The second view mentioned above of covering their heads and wrapping themselves with their outer garments, without need to cover their faces, is sufficient for making the distinction between free women and slaves. Therefore, it should be adopted so that no conflict between verses is entertained.
>
> In this way, each of the two verses addresses something different from the other. The first one requires women to cover themselves except their faces and hands, while the second requires covering the upper part of the body together with the woman's head and its adjacent area, meaning her forehead. The outer garment should also be wrapped around the body so as to distinguish free women in the way they cover themselves. This is what suits explanation of the Qur'anic general statements.

Ibn al-Qayyim gives a succinct statement explaining the right attitude when someone's view - regardless of his high status - is in conflict with a practice recommended by God's Messenger (peace be upon him). The hadiths included in the second chapter suggest that leaving women's faces uncovered was the predominant practice in Muslim society during the Prophet's lifetime and of his companions. I feel that these hadiths confirm that leaving women's faces uncovered is a Sunnah applied by the Prophet (peace be upon him). Ibn al-Qayyim said:

> What we believe in, as part of our faith, and the only way available to us in this connection is that if a hadith is authentically narrated and attributed to God's Messenger

(peace be upon him), with no other similarly authentic hadith abrogating it, then it is obligatory for us and the Muslim community to uphold and implement this hadith. Everything else should be discarded. We may not abandon such a hadith because someone else disagrees with it, whoever that person may be, whether it's the narrator or someone else. The narrator may forget the hadith, or it may escape him at the time when he is giving a ruling, or he may not be aware of its relevance to the question in hand, or he may give it an unsound interpretation thinking it in conflict with the hadith but in fact it is unrelated to the question itself, or he may take someone else's fatwa that disagrees with the hadith because he believes that the scholar who gave that fatwa is more knowledgeable than himself and that he only gave his fatwa on the basis of a better evidence. If all these possibilities are inapplicable, and there is no way to determine or even suggest that they are inapplicable, still the narrator is not infallible.

Distinctive attire for free women

The cloak is for distinction

God says: 'Prophet! Say to your wives, daughters and all believing women that they should draw over themselves some of their outer garments. This will be more conducive to their being recognized and not affronted. God is much-forgiving, ever-merciful.' (33: 59) This verse requires women to draw their cloaks or outer garments over themselves when they go out to attend to their needs. The reason is to distinguish them from slave women and such distinction was a deterrent against being approached with any sort of impropriety. This means that the requirement to wear an outer garment is to be fully dressed, which encourages respect and decency. The obligatory covering of what should be covered of one's body is achieved with any sort of garment that meets the conditions Islamic law states. We may cite the following texts as evidence that the purpose of wearing an outer garment, or a cloak, was to be in full dress and ensure distinction:

1. God says: 'This will be more conducive to their being recognized and not affronted.' The statement gives the purpose of drawing the outer garment over oneself, namely, that people in the street recognize such women as free women and no one molests them.
2. Umm Salamah narrated: 'When the verse saying "draw over themselves some of their outer garments" was revealed, Anṣārī women came out with their head covering looking like crows.' (Related by Abu Dāwūd)
3. Umm 'Aṭiyyah narrated: 'We were ordered to bring out the women having their period and virgin women to the prayer place on Eid days. They attend with the Muslim community, observe their supplication, but those having a period stay away from the prayer. One woman asked: "Messenger of God, a woman may not have an outer garment." He said: "Let her friend give her one of hers."'

In *Fayḍ al-Bārī*, al-Kashmīrī comments on this hadith: 'This gives us the meaning that wearing a cloak is required when a woman goes out.' He also says: 'If it is suggested that drawing the outer garment over oneself makes it unnecessary to draw one's head covering over one's bosom, I will say that drawing the outer garment is needed when the woman goes out, while the head covering should be drawn in all situations.'

In the hadith narrated by Umm 'Aṭiyyah, a woman asks the Prophet about one who has no outer garment. This implies that the outer garment was not an essential part of a woman's dress which is needed to cover her body. She only needs it when she goes out, particularly when going out at night to answer the call of nature, and when she goes out to join the congregational prayer. This means that it was part of the full dress code for free women when they went out. Needless to say, going to the mosque or to the place of the Eid Prayer with such attire is even more important. Besides, the outer garment helps a woman to be well covered when she bows or prostrates herself in prayer held in a public place frequented by men and women. While the outer garment is to give a woman the complete appearance of propriety when she goes out, still not all women have one, yet every woman needs clothing that covers her body fully when she is at home, in order to offer her prayers and also when she deals with men. As will be presently explained, such clothing consisted of a robe and a head covering and the like.

Feature 3: The adornment women may show

God says: 'Tell believing women... not to display their charms except what may ordinarily appear thereof.' (24: 31) Explaining this statement, books of commentary on the Qur'an say:

- *JĀMI' AL-BAYĀN* BY AL-ṬABARĪ

  That God says: 'not to display their charms...' means that they must not show such charms to people who are not their immediate relatives whom they are forbidden to marry. These charms, or adornments, are of two types: covered, such as anklets, bracelets, earrings and necklaces; and apparent. Scholars differ as to what is meant by the apparent in this verse. Some said that this refers to the apparent adornment of clothing. Others say that the adornments a woman is allowed to show includes kohl, rings whether having a stone or not and her face... Ibn 'Abbās said that 'what may ordinarily appear' refers to the kohl and rings. He is quoted as saying that 'the apparent includes the kohl and the cheeks.' Sa'īd ibn Jubayr said that it refers to the face and the hand, while 'Aṭā' said that it means the hands and the face. Qatādah said it is the kohl and rings. A further view from Ibn 'Abbās mentions that the apparent charms are the woman's face, the kohl in her eyes, the henna on her hands and her rings. These appear to a person who visits her at home. Mujāhid said it is the kohl, the henna and the rings. 'Āmir said that it is the kohl, the henna and the clothes. Ibn Zayd said that the adornment includes the kohl, the henna and the rings: this is what people said and this is seen by people. Al-Awzā'ī was asked about it and his answer stated the hands and the face. Al-Ḍaḥḥāk said it is the hand and the face. Others said that it refers to the face and clothes. Quoting al-Ḥasan, Yūnus said: 'The face and clothes.'

The more correct of all these views is the one that says it means 'the face and two hands' because this includes the kohl, rings, henna and colouring. We say that this is the more correct view because all scholars agree that every worshipper must cover the *'awrah* during prayer. Yet a woman uncovers her face and hands when she prays but she has to cover the rest of her body. Since this is unanimously agreed upon, it means that a woman may uncover what is not *'awrah* in front of men. What is not part of the *'awrah* is not forbidden to uncover. Since a woman may leave these uncovered, it follows that it is part of what God has excepted as he said: 'Except what may ordinarily appear thereof,' as all that is apparent.

The view chosen by al-Ṭabarī is based on a Fiqh argument. Yet what he says gives an important indication. His view on this point is a testimony for his own time. A type of dress is something that applies to the whole community and everyone knows. Had covering the face been obligatory, it would have been universally known during al-Ṭabarī's generation, i.e. the third century of the Islamic calendar. Indeed, all Muslim women would have known it and only a loose woman would disregard it.

❧ *Aḥkām al-Qur'an* by al-Jaṣṣāṣ (died 370 AH, 981 CE)
God says: 'Tell believing women... not to display their charms except what may ordinarily appear thereof.' (24: 31) Ibn 'Abbās, Mujāhid and 'Aṭā' are reported to have said that 'what may ordinarily appear' refers to what appears on the woman's face and hands, such as the reddish colour, henna and kohl....

This confirms that the woman's face and hands are not part of the *'awrah*, which must be covered. A woman prays with her face and hands uncovered. Had they been part of her *'awrah*, she would have had to cover them as she covers all her *'awrah*.

❧ *Al-Wajīz fī Tafsīr al-Qur'an al-'Azīz* by al-Wāḥidī (died 468 AH 1076 CE)
'What may ordinarily appear thereof' refers to clothes, kohl, rings and colouring. A woman may not uncover any part of her body except her face and hands up to the middle of her arms.

❧ *Ma'ālim al-Tanzīl fī al-Tafsīr* by al-Baghawī (died 516 AH, 1122 CE)
'What may ordinarily appear thereof' refers to apparent adornment. Scholars differ as to what such apparent adornment means. Sa'īd ibn Jubayr, al-Ḍaḥḥāk and al-Awzā'ī said that it is the woman's face and hands, while Ibn Mas'ūd said that it means her clothing. The concession to leave this uncovered is due to the fact that it is not part of the woman's *'awrah*, and that she is commanded to leave it uncovered when she prays.

❧ *Al-Kashshāf* by al-Zamakhsharī (died 528 AH, 1134 CE)
Adornment refers to what a woman wears of jewellery, kohl or red colouring. What is apparent of this, such as rings,

kohl and colour may be shown to non-relatives. 'What may ordinarily appear thereof' means what is habitually and naturally apparent, and what is, in the nature of things, visible.

- *Aḥkām al-Qur'an* by Abu Bakr ibn al-'Arabī (died 543 AH, 1149 CE)

  Scholars express three different views as to what apparent adornment means... The correct view is that it refers to what is worn on a woman's face and hands, because these two are left uncovered during prayer and consecration as part of these acts of worship. They are what habitually and ordinarily appear.

- *Al-Muḥarrar al-Wajīz fī Tafsīr al-Qur'an al-'Azīz* by Ibn 'Aṭiyyah (died 546 AH, 1152 CE)

  'What may ordinarily appear thereof...'. God makes an exception allowing what appears of a woman's adornment, and people have differed as to the extent of that... It appears to me, on the basis of the wording of the Qur'anic verse, that the Muslim woman is commanded not to display any of her charms and adornment and that she should ensure that it is not apparent. The exception then applies to what appears despite her effort, because of the need to make a necessary move or to repair something, etc. What appears in this way is exempt. In most cases, the face and hands are often uncovered, and these are uncovered in prayer. It behoves a woman with a pretty face to cover herself except in front of her relatives whom she cannot marry. The wording of the verse admits the understanding that she may show what is apparent of her adornment, but what we have said is strengthened by the need to take precautions and realize that people's morality has declined.

☙ *Zād al-Masīr fī ʿIlm al-Tafsīr* by Ibn al-Jawzī (died 596 AH, 1200 CE)

Seven views have been expressed about the meaning of 'what may ordinarily appear thereof'. One of them is that it refers to clothes... and the second is that it means the hand, ring and face... Justice Abu Yaʿlā said: 'The first view is more likely, and it is clearly stated by Ahmad who said that the apparent adornment means her clothes. Every part of her body is *ʿawrah*, even her finger nails... If someone asks why her prayer is not invalidated then when her face is uncovered, the answer would be that because covering her face is hard on her, it has been exempted.'

In response I say that if there is hardship in covering her face during prayer, the hardship is greater at other times. If she is to cover her face then, the time may be much longer than the prayer time. While Justice Abu Yaʿlā mentions this view as being the view of Imam Ahmad's Ḥanbalī School, a different view is given by al-Khiraqī in his *al-Mukhtaṣar* and by Ibn Qudāmah in his explanation of *al-Mukhtaṣar*. This other view may be summed up as the permissibility of uncovering the Muslim woman's face during prayer, and that her face is not part of her *ʿawrah*, during or outside prayer.

☙ *Al-Tafsīr al-Kabīr* by al-Rāzī (died 606 AH, 1210 CE)

Scholars differ as to the meaning of 'what may ordinarily appear thereof'. Of those who take the word *zīnah* to refer to the person of the woman, [giving its meaning as 'charms'], al-Qaffāl said that the verse refers to what appears of a person's body in ordinary situations. In women, this means the face and both hands... Therefore, they are ordered to cover what there is no need to uncover, while what is habitually and necessarily exposed has been allowed to uncover. Islam is easy and tolerant in what it requires. Since the exposure of the Muslim woman's face and hands is akin to necessity, scholars agree that they are not part of a woman's *'awrah*. As for the feet, uncovering them is not necessary. Hence, scholars differ as to whether they are part of the woman's *'awrah*.

- *Al-Jāmi' li-Aḥkām al-Qur'an* by al-Qurṭubī (died 671 AH, 1273 CE)

  As it is mostly the case with regard to a woman's face and hands that they are uncovered, habitually and in worship, as in prayer and hajj, the exception in the Qur'anic verse may be rightly taken as referring to them... This is stronger as it is more cautious and takes into account people's relaxed standards of morality. Therefore, a Muslim woman does not expose of her charms any part other than her face and hands. God guides to what is right and there is no God other than Him.

- *Anwār al-Tanzīl wa Asrār al-Ta'wīl* by al-Bayḍāwī (died 685 AH, 1287 CE)

  'What may ordinarily appear thereof' when she is doing her work, such as her clothes and ring... All a free woman's body is *'awrah*, which means that it is not permissible for anyone other than her husband and immediate relatives to see any part of it, except for necessity, such as medical treatment or giving testimony.

- *Lubāb al-Ta'wīl fī Ma'ānī al-Tanzīl* by al-Khāzin (died 725 AH, 1326 CE)

  'What may ordinarily appear thereof' refers to apparent adornment. Sa'īd ibn Jubayr, al-Ḍaḥḥāk and al-Awzā'ī said that it is the woman's face and hands, while Ibn Mas'ūd said that it means her clothing. The concession to leave this uncovered is due to the fact that it is not part of the woman's *'awrah*, and that she is commanded to leave it uncovered when she prays.

☙ *Gharā'ib al-Qur'an wa Raghā'ib al-Furqān* by al-Naisābūrī (died 728 AH, 1329 CE)

The free woman's *'awrah* in respect of a man includes all her body. He may not look at any part of her except her face and hands. She needs to leave her face uncovered when she sells and buys, and to put out her hand to take or give something. The hand includes both her palm and the back of her hand up to her elbow.

☙ *Al-Tashīl li-'Ulūm al-Tanzīl* by Ibn Juzzā al-Ghirnāṭī (died 741 AH, 1342 CE)

'Tell believing women... not to display their charms except what may ordinarily appear thereof'. The exception applies to what is apparent, which is normally seen when she moves or attends to what she needs, etc. Some say that 'what ordinarily appears' refers to clothes, which means that she must cover all her body. Others say that it means her clothes, face and hands. This is Mālik's view, because God permits her to uncover her face and hands in prayer. Abu Ḥanīfah adds her feet.

☙ *Al-Baḥr al-Muḥiṭ* by Abu Ḥayyān al-Andalusī (died 754 AH, 1355 CE)

God then says 'not to display their charms', and adds an exception of what may ordinarily appear. Apparent charms are overlooked because covering them causes hardship. A woman needs to do things with her own hands and she has to show her face, particularly if she is giving a testimony, during a court hearing and when entering into a marriage contract. She has to walk in the street, and this may necessitate that her feet are uncovered, particularly if she is poor. This is the meaning of 'except what may ordinarily appear thereof'. It means what is habitually uncovered and its normal condition is to be so. Moreover, light adornment is also overlooked... It may also be said that since in most cases the woman's face and hands are uncovered naturally and during worship, i.e. in prayer and hajj, it fits that the exception refers to them.

- *Tafsīr al-Qur'an al-'Aẓīm* by Ibn Kathīr (died 774 AH, 1374 CE)
  'Tell believing women... not to display their charms except what may ordinarily appear thereof'. This means that they may not show anything of their adornment except what cannot be hidden, such as clothes... However, Ibn 'Abbās and those who followed his lead wished to interpret the exception as meaning the woman's face and hands. This is the view held by the majority of scholars.

- *Tafsīr* Abu al-Su'ūd (died 951 AH, 1544 CE)
  Except what appears of her when she attends to her important tasks, such as her rings, kohl and colouring, etc. To cover these causes clear difficulty. It is also said that the term *zīnah* refers to its places, or what applies to natural charms and added makeup. What is excepted then is the face and hands, because these are not parts of the woman's *'awrah*.

- *Fatḥ al-Qadīr* by al-Shawkānī (died 1250 AH, 1834 CE)
  You well know that the apparent meaning of the Qur'anic wording is a prohibition of showing adornment, except what ordinarily appears of it, such as the woman's cloak and head covering, as well as similar articles that may be worn on hands and feet. If the 'adornment' refers to the place where it is worn, then the exception applies to the parts which a woman finds hard to cover, such as her hands and feet.

- *Nayl al-Murām min Tafsīr al-Aḥkām* by Siddiq Hasan Khan (died 1307 AH, 1890 CE)
  Scholars differ as to what is meant by the apparent *zīnah* or adornment... You well know that the apparent meaning of the Qur'anic wording is a prohibition of showing adornment,

except what ordinarily appears of it, such as the woman's cloak and head covering, as well as similar matter that may be worn on hands and feet. If the 'adornment' refers to the place where it is worn, then the exception applies to the parts which a woman finds hard to cover, such as her hands and feet.

☙ FROM IBN BĀDĪS'S HERITAGE, (DIED 1359 AH, 1940 CE)
As God says: 'not to show their charms', His words apply to those which are apparent and hidden, and as He added, 'except what may ordinarily appear thereof', the exception applies to what is apparent, while the hidden remained unlawful to uncover. The verse, thus, implies the prohibition of exposing the woman's neck, chest, legs, arms and all her body. It permits exposing the apparent, i.e. her face and hands. These are not part of her *'awrah*, as unanimously agreed upon.

We have, thus, presented what Qur'anic commentators say about the meaning of the Qur'anic statement: 'Tell believing women... not to display their charms except what may ordinarily appear thereof'. This exposition shows that 13 distinguished commentators on the Qur'an consider that the apparent charms that are permissible to be uncovered and seen by unrelated men are the woman's face and hands. These commentators are: al-Ṭabarī, al-Jaṣṣāṣ, al-Wāḥidī, al-Baghawī, al-Zamakhsharī, Ibn al-'Arabi, al-Fakhr al-Rāzī, al-Qurṭubī, al-Khāzin, al Naysābūrī, Abu Ḥayyān, Abu al Su'ūd and Ibn Bādīs.

These commentators who consider that the apparent adornment refers to clothing are Ibn al-Jawzī, al-Bayḍāwī and Ibn Kathīr. On the other hand, al-Shawkānī and Siddiq Hasan Khan add the hands and feet to clothing, while Ibn 'Aṭiyyah and Ibn Juzzā al-Ghirnāṭī mentioned the difference of views without expressing preference. Moreover, Ibn Kathīr mentions that the majority of scholars opt for the well-known view that the verse refers to the woman's face and hands.

When we say that 13 commentators prefer that the apparent *zīnah* refers to the face and hands we do not mean to say that the number indicates the right view. We merely want to say that the permissibility of exposing the face is not a newly invented view coined up by people who are infatuated by Western civilization and who consider covering women's faces merely an old tradition.

We may add that the reports mentioned by al-Ṭabarī and other scholars may have some question marks about their authenticity. However, regardless of this, they do not mention any verbal Sunnah, i.e. a hadith stated by the Prophet or a practical one he might have approved. They are no more than a preference stated by a scholar with regard to the meaning of the verse, and what he considers to be more likely the purpose of the exception and what fits with the required covering of women. Anyone may mention what is excepted by way of example, without limiting the exception to it. When we look at the different reports we find that every report mentions some of what may be excepted. Clothes, face, hands, kohl, rings and colouring are all aspects of charms or adornment that are apparent. Al-Ḥasan and ʿĀmir are right in their two reports quoted by al-Ṭabarī. Defining 'what may ordinarily appear', al-Ḥasan said: it is the face and clothes, while ʿĀmir said: it is the kohl, colouring and clothes.

Feature 4: The order to cover women's necks and chests

God says: 'Let them draw their head-coverings over their bosoms.' (24: 31)

'Urwah quotes ʿĀ'ishah as she said: 'May God bestow mercy on the early migrant women. When God revealed, 'Let them draw their head-coverings over their bosoms', they tore a portion of their shawls and covered their heads with it.' A different version says: 'They held their lower garments and tore portions of their ends and covered their heads with them.' (Related by al-Bukhari)

Ibn Ḥajar says in *Fatḥ al-Bārī*: 'Covered their heads with it' means that a woman put the cover over her head and brought it from her right side to put it over her left shoulder. Al-Farrā' said that in pre-Islamic days, a woman used to drop her head covering behind her back and expose the front. Women were thus ordered to cover themselves. The head covering is for women as a turban is for men.

Having explained these verses from Surahs 24 and 33, we need to make clear that the order to all Muslim women to 'draw over themselves some of their outer garments' (33: 59) speaks of a particular standard that applies to free women and that they should be clearly distinguished when they go out. This is to protect them from being affronted by ill-mannered men. Then the verses of Surah 24 provide an outline organizing how men and women see each other, so as to check the temptation that applies to both in all situations, inside and outside their homes. This begins by ordering both to lower their gaze: 'Tell believing men to lower their gaze.' (24: 30) 'And tell believing women to lower their gaze.' (24: 31)

The other aspect is to limit the scope of temptation caused by the woman's charms and adornment to the minimum. Women used to wear a head covering, but they would drop it behind their backs, exposing not only their faces and hands, but also their ears, necks and the top of their chests, with all the adornment a woman may wear on any of these parts of her body, including kohl on her eyes, henna on her hands, her earrings and necklace. As God says that women must not expose their charms and adornment 'except what may ordinarily appear thereof', this order means that only what naturally and ordinarily appears, according to recognized tradition, may remain uncovered. All the adornment we have just mentioned used to remain visible when a woman wore a long robe and a head covering. Hence, God revealed: 'Let them draw their head-coverings over their bosoms,' so that the Muslim woman covers with her head covering her ears, neck and top of her chest. Thus, the apparent charms and adornments are brought to a minimum, revealing only what is on a woman's face and hands, in addition to clothing. Had not the head covering been brought over the bosom, the ears, neck and top chest would remain apparent with their adornments. This is not the purpose of the Legislator. Had God, the Legislator, wanted women to cover their faces, he would have commanded that their head coverings be brought over their faces. This is what Ibn Ḥazm says: 'God ordered women to draw their head coverings over their bosoms. This is a clear text requiring that the *'awrah*, the neck and the chest be covered. It also means that it is permissible to leave the face uncovered. Nothing different may be said.'

Feature 5: To whom may a woman reveal her hidden charms?

God says: 'Let them draw their head-coverings over their bosoms and not display their charms to any but their husbands, or their fathers, or their husbands' fathers, or their sons, or their husbands' sons, or their brothers, or their brothers' sons, or their sisters' sons, or their womenfolk, or those whom they rightfully possess, or such male attendants as are free of physical desire, or children that are as yet unaware of women's nakedness. Let them not swing their legs in walking so as to draw attention to their hidden charms. Believers, turn to God in repentance, so that you may achieve success.' (24: 31)

This verse makes clear that a woman's hidden adornments may not be shown except to a certain number of people. This refers to the adornment which is not worn on a woman's face or hands. Thus, it includes earrings, necklaces, bracelets and anklets, i.e. the adornment a woman may wear on her head and limbs. The verse does not include paternal or maternal uncles among those who may see the hidden adornment of their nieces. Hence, commentators differ, with some considering them like the women's fathers and as such they may see such adornment. Others consider them like unrelated men who may not see such. Books of commentary quote a report attributed to ʿIkrimah and al-Shaʿbī saying that they discourage a woman taking off her head covering when she is with her paternal or maternal uncle, because they may describe her to their sons. The Sunnah, which explains what the Qur'an says, gives us the final word on this point. Al-Bukhari and Muslim relate the following two hadiths:

ʿAmrah bint ʿAbd al-Raḥmān reports that ʿĀ'ishah, the Prophet's wife, told her that God's Messenger (peace be upon him) was at her place when she heard a man seeking permission to enter Ḥafṣah's home. She said: 'Messenger of God, here is a man seeking entry into your home.' The Prophet said: 'I think he is so-and-so,' mentioning the name of Ḥafṣah's paternal uncle through breastfeeding. ʿĀ'ishah said: 'Had so-and-so, mentioning her own paternal uncle through breastfeeding, been alive, he could come into my home?' The Prophet said: 'Yes. Breastfeeding blocks marriages in the same way as birth.' (Related by al-Bukhari and Muslim)

ʿĀ'ishah narrated: 'Aflaḥ, Abu al-Quʿays's brother, sought permission to enter my home, after the decree of screening was revealed.' ʿĀ'ishah said: 'I thought that I must not admit Aflaḥ until I had obtained God's Messenger's permission. It was not Abu al-Quʿays who breastfed me, but his wife did.' ʿĀ'ishah said: 'When God's Messenger (peace be upon him) came in, I said: Messenger of God, Aflaḥ, Abu al-Quʿays's brother came and wished to enter, but I did not like to admit him until I had sought your permission.' The Prophet said: 'What stopped you from admitting him? He is your uncle.' I said: 'Messenger of God, it was not the man who breastfed me; it was Abu al-Quʿays's wife.' He said: 'Admit him; he is your uncle; this is amazing.' (Related by al-Bukhari and Muslim)

Fatḥ al-Bārī, Ibn Ḥajar's voluminous commentary on al-Bukhari's *Ṣaḥīḥ* anthology, includes a chapter with the following heading: 'Chapter: God says: "Whether you do anything openly or in secret, [remember that] God has full knowledge of everything. It is no sin for them [to appear freely] before their fathers, their sons, their brothers, their brothers' sons, their sisters' sons, their womenfolk, or such men slaves as their right hands possess. [Wives of the Prophet!] Always remain God-fearing; for God is witness to all things.'" (33: 54-5) Ibn Ḥajar then mentions the hadith speaking about Aflaḥ as narrated by 'Ā'ishah, highlighting the fact that it fits with the chapter heading, which includes the verse that says: 'It is no sin for them...' In the hadith the Prophet tells 'Ā ishah: 'Admit him, he is your uncle'. He says in another hadith: 'A paternal uncle is equal to one's father.' Thus, any objection claiming that the hadith does not fit with the chapter heading is refuted. It appears that al-Bukhari quotes this hadith at this particular place in response to anyone who discourages that a woman takes off her head covering when she is with her paternal or maternal uncles. This is a report related by al-Ṭabarī as narrated by Dāwūd ibn Abi Hind from 'Ikrimah and al-Sha'bī. They were asked: 'Why are paternal and maternal uncles not mentioned in this verse?' They said: 'Because they describe her to their sons.' Therefore, both discourage a woman taking off her head covering when she is with her uncle. The hadith narrated by 'Ā'ishah refutes their argument. This is an example of the subtleties of al-Bukhari's headings.

It is also reported: 'If it is said that paternal and maternal uncles are not mentioned in this verse, the answer is that they are implicitly referred to because a paternal uncle is like a father and a maternal uncle is like a mother.'

Al-Qurṭubī said: 'The majority of scholars are of the view that uncles, paternal and maternal, are the same as all other unmarriageable relatives. They may see what other such relatives may see.'

In *Fatḥ al-Qadīr* by al-Shawkānī we read: 'Uncles are not mentioned because they are treated in the same way as parents. Al-Zajjāj said:

"Paternal and maternal uncles are not mentioned because they may describe a woman to their sons. It is lawful for a woman to marry her paternal or maternal cousin. Therefore, it is discouraged that they see their niece's charms." This argument is very flimsy. A woman may be described to someone who can marry her by anyone who can see her, particularly her nephews and nieces. Likewise, other women may describe her to men. Yet this argument is not upheld. Thus, what al-Sha'bī and 'Ikrimah have said describing as discouraged, or *makrūh*, for a woman to uncover her head when she visits her paternal or maternal uncles.

Scholars differ about the meaning of 'their womenfolk' in the above-quoted verse (24: 31). Justice Abu Bakr ibn al-'Arabī says in his book *Aḥkām al-Qur'an*: 'Two views have been mentioned: one says that it refers to all women, and the other to women who believe. To my mind, the correct view is that it embraces all women.'

Ibn Qudāmah says in *al-Mughnī*: 'There is no difference between two Muslim women and one Muslim woman and the other non-Muslim, in the same way as there is no difference between two Muslim men and one Muslim man and another non-Muslim in as far as looking is concerned. Ahmad [ibn Ḥanbal] said: "Some people have suggested that a Muslim woman may not take off her head covering when she visits a Jewish or Christian woman. My own view is that a non-Muslim woman may not look at a Muslim woman's genitals and may not receive her child when she gives birth." Another view attributed to Ahmad is that a Muslim woman may not take off her head covering when she visits a non-Muslim, and may not enter a public bath with her. The same view is expressed by Makḥūl and Sulaymān ibn Mūsā on the basis of the verse that includes "or their womenfolk." The first view is more valid because unbelieving women, Jewish and others, used to visit the Prophet's wives and the Prophet's wives did not screen themselves, nor were they ordered to remain behind a screen... Moreover, the covering between men and women is meant for a purpose that does not apply between a Muslim and a non-Muslim woman. Hence, covering between them does not apply in the same way as such restrictions do not apply between Muslim and non-Muslim men. Covering and screening is determined only on the basis of a clear text or a valid analogy. Neither one applies in this case.'

Feature 6: Hiding leg adornments

God says: 'Let them not swing their legs in walking so as to draw attention to their hidden charms.' (24: 31)

Covering legs

Here are two hadith texts confirming that legs must be covered. Attention should be drawn to that whereby God's Messenger warns a woman against leaving her legs exposed, implying that it is obligatory to keep legs covered.

Abu Hurayrah narrated from 'Ā'ishah that the Prophet said: 'Let women drop their tail ends by a hand span.' 'Ā'ishah said: 'Then their legs may be exposed'. He said: 'Then an arm's length.' (Related by Ibn Mājah)

Uncovered feet

The ordinary clothing Arab women used to wear during the Prophet's lifetime indicate that it was natural that a woman's feet would appear when she walked in the street, whether she was wearing sandals or was bare-footed. Sandals leave parts of the feet exposed. Texts indicating this include:

Sa'īd ibn Jubayr narrated from Ibn 'Abbās: 'The first time women used belts on their waists was when Ismā'īl's mother used it to wipe off the traces of her feet so that Sarah could not trace her.' (Related by al-Bukhari)

Abu Nawfal narrated that Asmā' bint Abu Bakr said: 'By God, I am the woman with two belts. I used one to tie up the food of God's Messenger and Abu Bakr away from animals and the other is the indispensable belt women need.' (Related by Muslim)

Ibn Ḥajar said: A belt is what is used to tie [clothing] up at one's waist. Hagar used one, tying it up to her waist and escaped, drawing the tail end of her robe behind her so that Sarah could not trace her. He also said that this means that a woman would wear a robe and tie it up at her waist, lifting its middle. She then drops it down so that she is not tripped by its tail end.

Ibn Taymiyyah said: They used to drop their tail ends. Thus, when a woman walks, her feet may appear.

Going out bare-foot

To walk bare foot was normal for Bedouin women. However, sometimes it is caused by poverty. Umm Salamah, the Prophet's wife, mentions that when the lower garment was mentioned she said: 'How about women, Messenger of God?' He said: 'She drops it the length of a hand span.' Umm Salamah said: 'It will then leave parts of her exposed.' He said: 'Then she drops it by an arm's length, no more.' (Related by Mālik)

Explaining this hadith narrated by Umm Salamah, al-Baji said: 'This shows that it was not customary for Arabian women to wear stockings or *khuff* (i.e. inner light shoes). They used to wear sandals or walk bare-foot. To cover their legs they used to drop the tail end of their clothes, but God knows best.'

Abu Ḥayyān al-Andalusī said in *al-Baḥr al-Muḥīṭ*: 'A woman needs to walk in the street and her feet will be uncovered. This applies in particular to poor women.'

Going out wearing sandals

Some women believers used to go out wearing sandals. They had neither stockings nor shoes of any type. Abu Ḥanīfah said: 'A woman may be forced to have her feet exposed when she goes out, whether she walks bare-foot or wearing sandals. She may not have shoes.' Al-Bājī said: 'It was not customary for Arabian women to wear stockings or *khuff* (i.e. inner light shoes). They used to wear sandals.' Ibn Taymiyyah said: 'Women did not have *khuffs* or shoes.'

Some hadiths indicate the need to cover women's feet. One such hadith is narrated by Ibn 'Umar quoting God's Messenger (peace be upon him): 'On the Day of Judgement, God will not look at anyone who [in this life] drags his robe [behind him] in arrogance'. Umm Salamah asked: 'What should a woman do concerning her tail end?' The Prophet said: 'She drops it the length of a hand span'. Umm Salamah said: 'Then her feet will be exposed.' He said: 'She drops it by an arm's length, not more.' (Related by al-Tirmidhī)

This hadith refers to covering the Muslim woman's feet. However, when we look at it carefully in the light of the above-quoted hadiths mentioning Hagar and Asmā', we realize that it speaks about covering the lower part of the woman's legs, above her feet. The tail end of her robe may be long and may cover her feet when she is at home, not moving about. When she attends to her household errands or walks outside, she needs to use a belt on her waist, so that she is not tripped by her tail. In this case, her robe will be shorter in the front and her feet become exposed.

It should be considered that when a woman wears a dress that only shows her feet when she is standing still, then the lower parts of her legs and her anklets and other ornaments will be exposed if she moves about to lift or put something on the floor, or if she bows during prayer. Further, we believe that what is meant by the feet or the legs being exposed, as expressed in this and other hadiths, is a full exposure of the feet and the parts of the shins.

It is this part of the leg, not merely the feet, that most probably prompts the caution. This is further confirmed by the fact that when Umm Salamah alerted to the exposure, the Prophet said that women 'may drop [their tail ends] by an arm's length, not more.' What need is there for 'an arm's length'? If dropping the tail end by the length of a hand span covers the entire leg, leaving only the feet exposed, dropping it a couple of inches further would be enough to cover the woman's feet.

Further support of this understanding is provided by Ibn Taymiyyah who says: 'Women started to wear the *khuffs* later so that they would cover their legs when they go out. They do not wear these at home. Hence, they said: "Then their legs would be exposed." The point was how to cover a woman's legs. If a dress is ankle length, the woman's leg will be exposed when she walks.'

Other Fiqh scholars express the view that it is permissible to uncover the woman's feet. Al-Kamāl ibn al-Hammām, a leading Ḥanafī scholar says in his book *Fatḥ al-Qadīr*: 'The woman's *'awrah* is confirmed by the Prophet as he said: "The woman's [body] is *'awrah,*" yet certain parts of her body are definitely excepted. This is what is referred to as 'the test of exposure'. It certainly entails that the woman's feet are excepted as part of the test.'

Akmal al-Dīn Muhammad al-Bābartī writes in his book *Sharḥ al-'Ināyah 'ala al-Hidāyah*: 'Al-Ḥasan reports from Abu Ḥanīfah that the feet are not part of the *'awrah*. This is also al-Karkhī's view... A Muslim woman may not be able to wear the *khuffs*, and thus she is tested by exposing her feet when she walks bare-foot or wearing sandals. However, looking at a woman's feet does not arouse man's desire in the same way as looking at her face. If the woman's face is not *'awrah* despite arousing a strong desire, it is more so in the case of her feet.'

Feature 7: A concession for older women

God says: 'Such elderly women as are past the prospect of marriage incur no sin if they lay aside their [outer] garments, provided they do not make a showy display of their charms. But it is better for them to be modest. God hears all and knows all.' (24: 60)

This verse gives elderly women who are neither sought nor hope for marriage a concession, because there is no temptation in their case. The concession allows them to put off some of their outer garments. Thus, if such a woman is at home and some men enter her home, there is no harm if she meets them without covering her head, which is the normal case for other women. If she goes out, she need not wear a cloak.

To suggest that this verse means that such a woman no longer needs to wear a veil, i.e. *niqab* is valid only if the veil is obligatory to all women, and we have already explained that it is not so. This is further confirmed by the fact that Asmā' bint Abu Bakr went out with her face uncovered when she was an elderly woman. Had the veil been meant by the clothing that elderly women need not wear, she would not have taken it off, because God says in this verse, 'but it is better for them to be modest.' She would certainly have sought what was better for herself.

Further requirements

Having stated the features of women's attire, as mentioned in the Qur'an, we should add that the first condition, which is 'covering the woman's body except her face, hands and feet' entails further requirements concerning the type of clothing a woman wears to cover herself. In order for the cover to be appropriate, the woman's clothing should be opaque, non-transparent and loose so that they do not reveal her charms or show her body. True covering is not achieved without such qualities. God says that women believers must not expose their charms, and this is not a mere formality. It is not achieved by putting something over such charms. It requires full covering for a definite purpose which is preserving its importance, preventing temptation and helping men to lower their gaze. These must be achieved in order to consider that a Muslim woman has truly implemented God's order not to display her charms.

We need to add some clarification. It is not a condition that a woman's clothing must not describe any part of the woman's body. The Qur'anic verse orders women 'not to display their charms'. This means that what must not be described is her charms, and what may constitute temptation to men when its condition is shown or suggested. In this context we have a hadith narrated by Usāmah ibn Zayd: 'God's Messenger (peace be upon him) gifted me a thin opaque white garment which was part of what Diḥyah al-Kalbī had gifted him. I gave it to my wife to wear. God's Messenger asked me why I had not worn it. I told him that I gave it to my wife. He said: "Tell her to wear a vest under it, as I fear that it may describe the size of her bones."' What is meant by 'bones' in this instance is the apparent parts of her body, or charms. Needless to say, bones are not attractive, but the Prophet's usage is a subtle reference to her body. Another example of such usage is a hadith narrated by 'Abdullāh ibn 'Umar: 'Tamīm al-Dārī said to God's Messenger when he put on weight: "Shall I make a platform [i.e. *minbar*] to carry your bones?" The Prophet said: "Yes." He made him such a platform.' Another example is the hadith reported by Ibn Ḥazm: 'A fasting person who gazes at a woman until he can see the size of her bones invalidates his fast.'

Therefore, there is no problem with wearing clothes that show the size of some of her organs which have bones, such as her head, shoulders, feet, ankles and the lower parts of her legs, as long as these organs are covered with non-transparent clothing and what is shown of them does not display any charms. Fiqh scholars, such as Ibn Qudāmah and al-Nawawī make clear that a woman's clothes must not be transparent so as to show the colour of her *'awrah*, yet they only say that it is desirable that her cloak should be wide enough not to make her clothing show her figure.

In conclusion it is appropriate to quote the following hadith which gives a warning to women who wear what describes or reveal their charms, describing them as 'clothed naked.' Abu Hurayrah narrated that God's Messenger (peace be upon him) said: 'Two types of the dwellers of hell I was not shown: people who have whips like cows tails, using them to beat people and clothed naked women, leaning and tempting, with their heads like tilting humps. They do not enter heaven and they cannot even smell it, when its smell is recognized at such and such distance.'

CHAPTER III

Women's Faces Uncovered during the Prophet's Time

Note: Readers' attention is drawn to the fact that some of the Qur'anic and hadith evidence we cite here is not clear and direct in indicating what we are suggesting. However, their relevance to our point is clearly understood when they are taken within their broader context and when we see how scholars explained them.

One: Evidence from the Qur'an and its hadith explanation

The first verses to be cited in this connection are the ones commanding believers to lower their gaze. God says: 'Tell believing men to lower their gaze and to be mindful of their chastity. This is most conducive to their purity. God is certainly aware of all that they do. And tell believing women to lower their gaze and to be mindful of their chastity.' (24: 30–31)

In his commentary on these verses al-Shawkānī says in his book *Fatḥ al-Qadīr*: 'Ibn Mardawayh relates a hadith narrated by 'Alī ibn Abi

Ṭālib: "A man was going along some road in Madinah during the Prophet's lifetime when he saw a woman and looked at her. She also looked at him. Satan whispered to each of them that the other only looked admiring you. The man was walking alongside a wall as he looked at the woman, he inadvertently faced the wall [and hit it] cutting his nose. He thought: 'By God, I shall not wash off the blood until I have seen God's Messenger and told him what has happened to me.' He went to him and told him his story. The Prophet said: 'This is punishment for your sin.'""

Ibn 'Abd al-Barr said: 'It is permissible for everyone to look at these (i.e. her face and hands) without harbouring ill thoughts. A look with desire is different. In fact to intently gaze at her body, covered with her clothes, is forbidden, let alone casting such a look at her uncovered face.'

Ibn al-Qayyim said: 'God has commanded us to lower our gaze', although it sees the beauty of creation and leads to admiring God's creation. The order is to counter the arousing of desire that may lead to what is forbidden.

We may add that these two verses implicitly inform us that in the majority of cases, Muslim women did not cover their faces. The same is indicated by another Qur'anic verse: 'God is well aware of the most stealthy glance, and of everything the heart would conceal.' (40: 19) Ibn Ḥajar quotes al-Karmānī who says in explanation that God knows a glance stealthily cast at what is forbidden. Ibn 'Abbās is quoted by Ibn Abi Ḥātim as saying that the verse refers to a man casting a look at a pretty woman as she passes across, or enters a house where she happens to be. He would lower his gaze when he was aware that others had noticed him.

The question we ask is how could a man admire a woman's beauty when she passed by unless it was women's habit to leave their faces uncovered? The hadiths urging lowering one's gaze and warning against staring intently at women are numerous. Here are some examples:

Abu Saʿīd al-Khudrī quotes the Prophet (peace be upon him): 'Do not sit by the road side.' People said: 'We cannot do without that. These are our places where we sit and chat together.' He said: 'If you have to, then give the road its due rights.' They asked: 'What is the right of the road?' He said: 'Lowering one's gaze, removing harm, returning greeting, enjoining what is right and forbidding evil.' (Related by al-Bukhari and Muslim)

Ibn Ḥajar said: 'The hadiths explain the cause of the Prophet's order not to sit by the road side. What this may involve is the temptation that results when young women pass by and what looking at them may entail. The women are not ordered not to go out to attend to their needs at any particular time.'

Ibn ʿAbbās said: I know nothing that is akin to minor sin than what Abu Hurayrah has narrated from the Prophet (peace be upon him). He said: 'God has assigned every human being his share of fornication: the eye's fornication is by looking; the tongue's by speech; the man wishes and feels the desire; and the genital confirms all this or disproves it.' (Related by al-Bukhari and Muslim)

Is it possible that all these reminders and warnings are meant to prevent looking at the clothes or outer garments women wear? Could they be meant as warning against looking at something of a woman's hidden charms or ornaments that have been accidentally or unintentionally exposed, which rarely happens anyway?

God says: 'Tell believing men to lower their gaze.' (24: 30) The very statement implies that there is something normally seen of a woman and requires that a man should not stare hard at it. To have such a statement, giving this order, means that the woman was not like a ghost, covered in blackness, or some other dark colour, with nothing of her body visible. Likewise, there was something in the appearance of man that required women to lower their gaze: 'Tell believing women to lower their gaze.' (24: 31) This means that the attraction is mutual between men and women. Both need to lower their gaze so as not to stare intently at what appears of the other person's body.

Had Islam commanded women to cover their faces, there would be no need to order men to lower their gaze, and to re-emphasize the order on several occasions. There would be nothing to lower their gaze at. We would only have had the order given to women to lower their gaze, because men would be the only ones to show their faces, and more than their faces at times. Yet the command to lower one's gaze is given to both men and women in an equal way. Such equality means that both men and women could see of the other what would be enough to tempt them, and the minimum that is common to both is the face and hands. While this is the maximum that a woman is allowed to uncover, it is the minimum a man normally exposes.

Some may claim that it is better to shut the door of temptation fully and completely by covering women's faces. Could this apply in reverse, and require men to cover their faces so as to shut the door of temptation to women? This applies if such people want to remove temptation totally from both men and women, not from only one of the two sexes.

This attitude proves two points. The first is that there is an arbitrary and illogically persistent attempt to try to totally shut the door of temptation between men and women. This is evidenced by the fact that it is an impossible task. The other point is that there is an attempt to keep women in a weaker position on the one hand and there is an unhealthy feeling of jealousy among men prompting them to claim that only a woman's husband and her immediate unmarriageable relatives may see her face.

The second Qur'anic evidence is the verse that says: 'You [Muhammad] are not permitted to take any further wives, nor to exchange these for other wives, even though you are attracted by their beauty.' (33: 52)

This Qur'anic verse states that God's Messenger (peace be upon him) could not get married again even if he were attracted by the beauty of a particular woman. Yet, how could he to be attracted by a woman's beauty if he could not see her face? It should be borne in mind that seeing a woman in this case is different from that of a person who has a clear intention to make a marriage proposal to her. When such an intention is declared, a woman who habitually wears the veil or *niqab* should take it off. Seeing, as the verse implies, is what happens casually and in all situations where men meet women. A man may be attracted by a woman's beauty. In this context, al-Jaṣṣāṣ says: 'He will not be attracted by their beauty unless he has seen their faces.'

As the Qur'anic verse mentions the possibility that the Prophet might be attracted by the beauty of some women when he saw them casually, several hadiths mention that this is also possible for all men, due to the fact that women normally have their faces uncovered when they meet men or pass in front of them. Jābir mentions that he heard the Prophet (peace be upon him) say: 'If any of you sees a woman and is attracted by her, he should go to his wife and have intercourse with her. That is enough to remove what he has experienced.' (Related by Muslim)

ʿAbdullāh ibn Masʿūd said: 'A woman is *ʿawrah*. A woman may go out of her home and she is fine. Satan looks at her and says to her: You shall certainly be admired by everyone you pass by...' (Related by al-Ṭabarānī)

A third evidence from the Qur'an is given in the following verse: 'You will incur no sin if you give a hint of a marriage offer to [widowed] women or keep such an intention to yourselves. God knows that you will entertain such intentions concerning them. Do not, however, plight your troth in secret; but speak only in a decent manner. Furthermore, do not resolve on actually making the marriage tie before the prescribed term [of waiting] has run its course. Know well that God knows what is in your minds, so have fear of Him; and know that God is much-forgiving, clement.' (2: 235)

In his commentary on this verse, al-Ṭabarī includes several reports by the Prophet's companions and their successors on how one may 'give a hint of a marriage offer' to a woman who is observing a waiting period after her husband's death or after she has been irrevocably divorced. Ibn 'Abbās said: 'The man may say: I would love to have a woman who has such-and-such qualities.' Mujāhid said that he may say to her: 'You are pretty and you will have no shortage of proposals. You shall certainly be fine.' Al-Qāsim ibn Muhammad said: 'A man may say something on the lines of: I would love to be with you; I am keen to serve your interests; I am full of admiration of you; etc.'

That a man visits a woman who is observing a waiting period indicates that her face is uncovered. Had she been used to covering her face, both the man and the woman herself would be ill at ease with such a visit. If the visit is coupled with words like, 'You are pretty,' and 'I am full of admiration of you,' this confirms that her face is more likely not to be covered. We have already mentioned that Islam prohibits wearing makeup such as kohl during the waiting period, so that men do not see her wearing her adornments. Giving a hint of a prospective offer of marriage is one of the causes that allow men to see women during the latter's waiting period. Moreover, a person who intends to make an offer of marriage is recommended to look at the woman's face, because this increases the chance of having a smooth relationship, as God's Messenger says. How can a man see a woman to whom he hints of a marriage offer unless her face is uncovered? The woman would not deliberately go out of her way to uncover her face when there is no previous indication that the man is entertaining the idea of proposing to her.

Two: Evidence from the Sunnah

The first evidence from the Sunnah is the hadith which requires that prostration in prayer should place one's seven bones on the ground, including the forehead and the nose. Ibn ʿAbbās said that the Prophet (peace be upon him) said: 'I have been commanded to do my prostration on seven bones: the forehead – and he pointed with his hand to his nose – the two hands, the two knees and the toes.' (Related by al-Bukhari) Another version related by al-Nasāʾī mentions: 'He placed his hand on his forehead and brought it over his nose, saying that this is one.'

Al-Bukhari enters this hadith in the chapter, 'Prostration on the nose'. Ibn Ḥajar says in his commentary: 'Ibn al-Mundhir confirms that the Prophet's companions were unanimous that placing only one's nose on the floor is invalid, but the majority of scholars are of the view that to do the prostration on one's forehead, without one's nose, is sufficient. However, al-Awzāʿī, Ahmad, Isḥāq and the Mālikī scholar Ibn Ḥabīb as well as other scholars express the view that including both the forehead and the nose is a duty. Al-Shāfiʿī is of the same view.

Al-Shāfiʿī says in his voluminous book, *al-Umm*: 'The perfect way of doing the prostration, with its obligatory and recommended parts, is that a person places on the floor his forehead, nose, two palms, two knees and two feet. If he prostrates himself on his forehead, but not his nose, I dislike this, although his prostration is valid.'

Ibn ʿAbd al-Barr says in *al-Tamhīd*: 'Women are commanded to uncover their faces and hands during prayer.'

In his rulings, or fatāwā, Ibn Taymiyyah says: 'To order a woman to cover her hands during prayer is to go too far. The hands are prostrated in the same way as the face is prostrated.'

To claim that the *'awrah* during prayer is different from other situations is going far in the wrong. We shall outline the evidence confirming this in Chapter 5.

If, for argument's sake, we consider this claim to be right, what should she do when she prays in a mosque? It is well known that many Muslim women used to attend the congregational prayer in the mosque with the Prophet. Should a woman who is praying in a mosque uncover her face because she is praying? Or, should she cover it so that she is not seen by men? Moreover, had it been common practice that the female companions of the Prophet used to cover their faces, we would have had reports that they also used to take off their veils and uncover their faces when they prayed. It is to be noted that women used to attend the Prophet's Mosque for prayer throughout the period when the Prophet lived in Madinah.

A second evidence given in the Sunnah is the Prophet's order that a person who wants to make an offer of marriage should look at the woman he intends to marry. Abu Hurayrah narrated: 'I was with the Prophet (peace be upon him) when a man came over and told him that he was marrying an Anṣārī woman. The Prophet asked him: "Have you seen her?" The man said: "No." The Prophet said: "Go and look at her; the Anṣār have something in their eyes."' (Related by Muslim) Jābir mentions that God's Messenger (peace be upon him) said: 'If any of you proposes to marry a certain woman and he can see of her what encourages him to marry her, he should do so.' (Related by Abu Dāwūd)

Abu Isḥāq al-Shīrāzī, a Shāfi'ī scholar, said: 'If a man intends to marry a woman, he may look at her face and hands. He should not look at any part other than her face and hands because that is *'awrah.'* Ibn Qudāmah, a Ḥanbalī scholar, said: 'The man making a proposal may look at the woman's face, because it is the centre of her charms, the place to look and it is not *'awrah.'*

The Sunnah gives us a third evidence in the form of prohibiting a woman in mourning to wear any adornments. Umm 'Aṭiyyah narrated that the Prophet said: 'It is not lawful for a woman who believes in God and the Last Day to be in mourning for more than three days, except for her husband. She may not wear kohl, wear colourful clothes except the *'aṣb* type,[2] and may not wear perfume.' (Related by al-Bukhari and Muslim)

Ibn Qudāmah said that mourning requires avoiding adornments and whatever may be attractive to men. It is obligatory during the woman's waiting period after her husband's death. She is forbidden to apply kohl because it is mentioned in the hadith and it improves her looks. Also, she must not wear jewellery because it makes her more attractive.

Ibn Rushd said: 'Scholars who apply the rulings concerning a widow to one who is observing a waiting period after being divorced rely on the meaning. It appears that mourning means that she should not look attractive to men.'

We may add that men cannot consider a woman who is observing a waiting period attractive unless her face is uncovered and she is wearing some adornments.

Ibn al-Qayyim said: 'It is forbidden for a woman in mourning to apply red and other colouring, paint her hands, apply henna or whitening

2. *'Aṣb* clothes were imported from Yemen. Its raw material is tied up and dyed before it is weaved. It thus turns out to be partly coloured.

to her skin. The Prophet has mentioned the red colouring to alert to the prohibition of all these types which are more adorning and attractive, and more contrary to the purpose of mourning.' We note that Ibn al-Qayyim mentions certain types of adornments as being 'more attractive'. We ask: are they more attractive to other women, to the woman's immediate relatives whom she cannot marry, or to other men generally? They will not be more attractive to men unless the woman uncovers her face and she is seen with such adornments on her face.

Had it been the case that women believers generally used to cover their faces from men in ordinary situations, uncovering only one eye when there was some urgent need, there would be no reason to fear that men would see the face of a woman in mourning and be attracted to her. How could they be attracted when they could see nothing that could be construed as attractive?

The fourth evidence from the Sunnah relies on the fact that the Mothers of the Believers, i.e. the Prophet's wives, were distinguished by being screened, and when they needed to go out they were distinguished by covering their faces. Free women were distinguished by uncovering their faces, while slave women were distinguished by wearing no head coverings.

- Anas narrated: 'The Prophet stopped for three days between Khaybar and Madinah, so as to consummate his marriage to Ṣafiyyah bint Ḥuyay... Muslims said: "If he screens her, she is one of the Mothers of the Believers, but if he does not, then she is one he possesses, i.e. a slave."' (Related by al-Bukhari and Muslim)

This hadith shows that the Prophet's companions were well aware of the distinction of the way the Prophet's women were covered. His wives were covered by being screened while his slaves were covered by long clothes, according to the common practice that distinguished free women from slaves by the way both dressed.

- Jābir ibn Samurah narrated that a man accused Sa'd ibn Abi Waqqāṣ.... Sa'd said: 'My Lord, if this person is lying, give him a long life in poverty and expose him to tests.' 'Abd al-Malik ibn 'Umayr, who belonged to the *tābi'īn* generation said: 'I saw him when his eyebrows had dropped over his eyes in his very old age, yet he would still wink at maids as they passed in the street.' (Related by al-Bukhari)

The hadith implies that slave maids were distinguished in the way they covered themselves during the *tābi'īn* time. How else can we understand that the man only winked at slave maids and not at free women?

- Mālik mentions in *al-Muwaṭṭa'* that he learnt that 'Umar ibn al-Khaṭṭāb saw a slave woman belonging to his son 'Abdullāh wearing the same sort of clothes free women used to wear. 'Umar went into his daughter Ḥafṣah's home. He said to her: 'I have seen your brother's maid walking among people, wearing the same type as free women's clothes.' 'Umar objected [to her behaviour].

The report mentions that the woman wore the same sort of clothes free women wore. Had it been the case that free women normally covered their faces in public, this would imply that the slave woman would have covered her face. In this case, 'Umar would not have recognized her as his son's maid.

- 'Umar used to hit a slave woman if she wore a head covering. He would say to her: 'Are you, woman, adopting the style of free women?'

- 'Umar hit a slave belonging to Anas's family when he saw her wearing a head cover. He said to her: Uncover your head; do not imitate free women.

These reports of 'Umar and his orders to slave women to keep their heads uncovered so that they would be distinguished from free women are relevant to the point under discussion. Had it been the practice of free women to cover their faces, slave women would have been distinguished if they only uncovered their faces. Muslims would not have required slave women to uncover their heads, because that would leave more of the body of the woman exposed, adding to the temptation.

The fifth evidence from the Sunnah is that women used to go out with their faces uncovered to join the congregation of Fajr Prayer.

'Ā'ishah narrated: 'Believing women used to attend the Fajr Prayer with God's Messenger, covering their heads with their shawls, then return home when the prayer had finished. No one could recognize them in the darkness.' (Related by al-Bukhari and Muslim) Another hadith gives the same meaning but speaks about men. Al-Haythamī related in *Majma' al-Zawā'id* that 'Alī ibn Abi Ṭālib said: 'We used to pray with God's Messenger (peace be upon him) and then leave. We could not recognize one another.'

'Ā'ishah, the Mother of the Believers, is speaking here of women in general, not a particular woman, and she says that they were unrecognizable because of the darkness, not because of covering their faces. This means that women in general uncovered their faces.

To claim that this was before the command of screening given to the Prophet's wives provides no counter argument. The phraseology of the hadith implies that this was the normal practice over a long time:

'Believing women used to attend the Fajr Prayer.' It is not limited to any particular time. Had this practice been abrogated when the order of screening was given, 'Ā'ishah would have mentioned this.

Evidence number six from the Sunnah concerns an orphan girl whose guardian finds her attractive and wants to marry her.

'Urwah mentions that he asked 'Ā'ishah about the meaning of the verse which says: 'If you fear that you may not deal fairly by the orphans, you may marry of other women as may be agreeable to you.' (4: 3) She answered: 'Nephew, this refers to an orphan girl being brought up by her guardian. He is attracted by her beauty and wealth but wishes not to pay her a full dowry. This order is given that they must not marry such girls unless they pay them their full dowry.' (Related by al-Bukhari)

Needless to say, an orphan girl living with her guardian in the same home cannot continuously cover her face. Moreover, the hadith clearly mentions that the guardian is attracted by her beauty.

A clear permission that a woman may leave her face and hands uncovered is our seventh evidence from the Sunnah. 'Ā'ishah narrated that 'Asmā' bint Abu Bakr entered God's Messenger's home wearing thin clothes. The Prophet turned away from her and said to her: 'Asma', when a woman has attained puberty, it is not permissible that any part of her body be seen, except this and this, pointing to his face and hands.' (Related by Abu Dāwūd) Abu Dāwūd said: 'This hadith is *mursal*, because Khālid ibn Durayk did not meet 'Ā'ishah.'[3]

---

3. A hadith is graded as *mursal* if there is a gap between narrators. In this case Khālid who belonged to the *tābi'īn* generation is reporting from 'Ā'ishah without having met her. A hadith of this type is considered 'poor in authenticity', unless further evidence strengthens it, as is the case here.

In verifying this hadith to assess its grade, Shaykh Nāṣir al-Dīn al-Albānī[4] said: 'Sa'īd ibn Bashīr, one of the narrators in its chain of transmission is classified as 'weak', as stated by Ibn Ḥajar in *al-Taqrīb*. However, the hadith is reported in other forms which confirm it. Al-Bayhaqī gives the hadith an added strength in another way. He first reports 'Ā'ishah's hadith and adds what Ibn 'Abbās and others said explaining the meaning of the woman's charms that may be uncovered and referred to in the Qur'anic verse by the phrase, "except what ordinarily appears thereof." They say that this refers to the face and hands. Al-Bayhaqī then adds: 'In addition to this *mursal* hadith we have the statements of the Prophet's companions explaining what God has permitted to be seen of apparent charms and adornment. Thus, the statement becomes more solid. In his *Tahdhīb Sunan al-Bayhaqī*, al-Dhahabī expresses the same opinion. The Prophet's companions to whom he refers are 'Ā'ishah, Ibn 'Abbās and Ibn 'Umar. They say that the apparent adornment or charms are the face and the hands. He adds: 'We have reported the same meaning from 'Aṭā' ibn Abi Rabāḥ and Sa'īd ibn Jubayr. Likewise, it is also al-Awzā'ī's view.'

Shaykh Nāṣir al-Dīn al-Albānī enters this hadith narrated by 'Ā'ishah in his selection of the authentic hadiths in Abu Dāwūd's *Sunan*, stating that it is 'authentic'. Moreover, Ibn Qudāmah mentions in his book, *al-Mughnī*, a different version of the same hadith narrated by 'Ā'ishah, adding that Ahmad upholds this hadith as evidence.

Had covering the face by a veil or something else been a good practice of Muslim women generally, the Prophet would have encouraged Asmā', who was Abu Bakr's own daughter and al-Zubayr's wife, to do the same and cover her face. It would have been more fitting for her.

Further strengthening of this hadith, narrated by 'Ā'ishah, is provided by the evidence and other indications we mention in this

4. A leading Hadith scholar of the twentieth century.

chapter and the following one, provided in the Qur'an and the Sunnah in its verbal and approval versions.

Three: Evidence provided by several texts

Evidence 1: Texts stating that the Prophet's wives uncovered their faces before they were told to screen

Before we cite the relevant hadiths we need to understand that covering women's faces was known among Arab women in pre-Islamic days. This is evidenced by the mention of the *niqab* and the *burqa*ʿ in the poetry of that period. Both these Arabic words mean the veil.

- Anas narrated: 'During the Battle of Uhud people deserted the Prophet (peace be upon him)... I saw 'Ā'ishah bint Abu Bakr and Umm Sulaym. Both lifted their skirts and I could see their anklets. They quickly jerked waterskins on their backs and poured the water into people's mouths, then returned fast to fill them again and moved forward to pour it into people's mouths.' (Related by al-Bukhari and Muslim)
- Anas ibn Mālik narrated: 'I am the one who knows about this verse [ordering the *ḥijāb*] best. When Zaynab bint Jaḥsh was wed to God's Messenger (peace be upon him), she was with him at home. He prepared food and invited people. They sat conversing. (In Muslim's version: His wife turned her face to the wall.) Al-Ismāʿīlī added: 'Zaynab was seated to one side at home. She was a pretty woman.' The Prophet went out and came back more than once while the people continued in their conversation. God then revealed the verse that says: 'Believers! Do not enter the Prophet's homes, unless you are given leave, for a meal without waiting for its proper time. But when you are invited, enter; and when you have eaten, disperse without lingering for the sake of mere talk. Such behaviour might give offence to the Prophet, and yet he might

feel too shy to bid you go. God does not shy of stating what is right. When you ask the Prophet's wives for something, do so from behind a screen.' (33: 53) Thus the screening was ordered. The people left.' (Related by al-Bukhari and Muslim)

- 'Ā'ishah narrated a long hadith with details of the false accusation against her. In this hadith, she says: 'Ṣafwān ibn al-Mu'aṭṭal al-Sulamī al-Dhakwānī was left behind the army. He started moving early at night and reached the place where I was in the morning. He could see the black shape of a sleeping person. He came over to me and recognized me. He used to see me before we were ordered to be screened.' (Related by al-Bukhari and Muslim)

The first hadith indicates that 'Ā'ishah was not covering her face, because Anas recognized her as she was with Umm Sulaym [his mother] during the Battle of Uhud. The second hadith indicates that Zaynab bint Jaḥsh did not cover her face at the time, but her modesty made her sit facing the wall. Needless to say, a bride is normally well adorned when her wedding takes place. The third hadith states in the clearest and most expressive of forms that 'Ā'ishah did not cover her face before the screening order. Ṣafwān ibn al-Mu'aṭṭal used to see her, with her face uncovered. Otherwise, he would not have recognized her.

To explain the import of these texts we may say that the veil or *niqab* was a type of dress used by some Arab women before Islam. Had it been an essential means of safeguarding women, emphasizing their chaste characters and maintaining their modesty, it would have behoved the Prophet's wives to wear it, because only the highest standard of chastity and modesty suited them. As the texts clearly indicate, in the most expressive way, one of them was seen by men as she did not wear the veil before they were ordered to remain behind a screen. The same was the case of many of the highly virtuous female companions of the Prophet, as we will presently explain.

We can thus clearly state two points: the first is that using a veil to cover one's face was merely a type of clothing used by some Arab women. It indicated an aspect of luxury along with the fact that it was a cover. The other point is that using a veil was not common practice in the Islamic society of Madinah. If used at all, this was in rare cases. Neither the Prophet's wives nor the most virtuous female companions of the Prophet used it. Moreover, most of the reports that speak of covering women's faces are clearly lacking in authenticity.

Texts showing that the Prophet's wives covered their faces after the *ḥijāb* order:

From the two *Ṣaḥīḥ* anthologies of al-Bukhari and Muslim:

- ʿĀ'ishah narrated: 'Sawdah went out after the *ḥijāb* order for something she needed. She was a big woman (one version says she was tall, and another says that she was taller than other women). She would be recognized by anyone who knew her. ʿUmar ibn al-Khaṭṭāb saw her and said: "Sawdah, you cannot be unrecognized by us. Take care how you go out."' (Related by al-Bukhari and Muslim)
- In her long hadith giving the details of the false accusation against her. ʿĀ'ishah narrated: 'I went with God's Messenger (peace be upon him) on this expedition after the *ḥijāb* order was revealed... Ṣafwān ibn al-Muʿaṭṭal was left behind the army. He started moving early at night and reached the place where I was in the morning. He could see the black shape of a sleeping person... I woke up as he said *innā lillāh wa innā ilayhi rājiʿūn* as he recognized me... I covered my face with my cloak...' (Related by al-Bukhari and Muslim)

We commented earlier on her saying in this hadith 'He recognized me when he saw me as he used to see me before we were ordered to be screened.' We said that this is the clearest and most expressive statement that the Prophet's wives did not cover their faces before they were ordered to be screened. We now comment on her added statement: 'I woke up as he said *innā lillāh wa innā ilayhi rāji'ūn* as he recognized me... I covered my face with my cloak'. This is the clearest and most expressive statement that the Prophet's wives covered their faces after the *ḥijāb* order.

- Anas narrated: 'The Prophet stopped three days between Khaybar and Madinah so as to have his wedding with Ṣafiyyah bint Ḥuyay... When he was about to move, he prepared her place behind him and placed the screen between her and the people.'
- 'Aṭā' narrated: '... The Prophet's wives used to go out masked at night...' ('Masked' means wearing a veil to cover their faces or bringing the end of their cloaks over their faces if they were in a state of consecration.) (Related by al-Bukhari)

The Prophet's wives maintained covering their faces after the verse commanding them to be screened was revealed. However, this was a special requirement as a follow up to that order. None of the women believers shared this requirement with them. We will discuss the applicability of the *ḥijāb* to the Prophet's wives only in the second chapter of Volume 5.

Evidence 2: The Prophet's female companions uncovered their faces after the Prophet's wives were ordered to be screened

1. From the two *Ṣaḥīḥ* anthologies of al-Bukhari and Muslim:

- Muslim al-Qurrī said: 'I asked Ibn 'Abbās about the *tamattu'* method of hajj, and he approved it. Ibn al-Zubayr used to order people not to do it. [Ibn 'Abbās] said: Here is Ibn al-Zubayr's mother (Asmā' bint Abu Bakr) and she narrates that God's Messenger approved of it. Go and ask her. We visited her and found her a big, blind woman. She said: "God's Messenger (peace be upon him) approved of it."'

It may be said that at this time, Asmā' was an elderly woman and such women were exempt from wearing the veil. In answer, we say that God says in reference to such elderly women: 'But it is better for them to be modest.' (24: 60) Who is more keen to be modest and seek what is better than Asmā'? This, if it is correct to say that women who are not elderly are required to cover their faces.

Zaynab, 'Abdullāh ibn Mas'ūd's wife, reports: 'As I was in the mosque, I saw the Prophet addressing women and saying to them: "Give to charity, even though you may have to give of your jewellery." Zaynab used to support her husband and some orphans under her care. She said: '... I went to the Prophet and I found at his door a woman from the Anṣār having come to ask the same question I wanted to ask. Bilāl came by. We said to him: Ask the Prophet whether it is acceptable that I pay my charity [i.e. zakat] to support my husband and the orphans under my care. We told him not to tell the Prophet who we were. Bilāl went in and put our question to the Prophet. The Prophet asked him who we were. Bilāl said: "Zaynab." The Prophet asked: "Which Zaynab?" He said: "'Abdullāh's wife." (al-Nasā'ī adds: and Zaynab of the Anṣār). The Prophet said: "Yes it does. She indeed earns two rewards: one for doing a kindness to relatives and one for her charity."' (Related by al-Bukhari and Muslim)

Had it not been the common practice that women did not cover their faces and that men necessarily recognized them, God's Messenger (peace be upon him) would not have asked Bilāl who they were, and he would not have asked: 'Which Zaynab?' Bilāl could not have answered: "'Abdullāh's wife."

- Subay'ah bint al-Ḥārith, a companion of the Prophet, reports that she was married to Sa'd ibn Khawlah, but he died during the Prophet's pilgrimage. Only a short while after that she gave birth to her child. When she regained her strength, she started to wear make-up expecting a proposal. (In the version related by Ahmad: she wore kohl, henna and put on a good appearance.) Abu al-San'bil ibn Ba'kak came to her and said: "How come you are adorned expecting a proposal, hoping to get married? By God, you cannot get married before the lapse of four months and ten days [after your husband's death]." Subay'ah said: When he said this to me, I put on my clothes in the evening and went to God's Messenger (peace be upon him) and I asked him about this. He told me that I have finished my waiting period when I gave birth and he left it up to me to get married if I wished.' (Related by al-Bukhari and Muslim)

This is the case of an early companion of the Prophet who migrated with him, and she was married to another companion who took part in the Battles of Badr and Uḥud, the Encounter of the Moat and al-Ḥudaybiyah. Shortly after she regained her strength after giving birth, she adorned herself so that she would invite a proposal of marriage. A man, who was also a companion of the Prophet, entered her home and noticed how she adorned herself, wearing kohl and henna. He took issue with her because he thought that she had not finished her waiting period.

- Fāṭimah bint Qays, a woman from the early Muhājirīn, reports: 'My husband Abu 'Amr ibn Ḥafṣ ibn al-Mughīrah sent me 'Ayyash ibn Abi Rabī'ah to inform me that he had divorced me. He sent with him five *ṣā's* of dates and five of barley. [The *ṣāʿ* was a measure equal to a little more than two kilograms.] I said to him: Is this all my maintenance? Am I not to observe my waiting period in your home? He said: "No." I put on my clothes and went to see the Prophet. He asked me how many times I was divorced. I said: Three. He said: "He is right. You cannot claim maintenance. You can observe your waiting period at your cousin's home, Ibn Umm Maktūm. Since he is a blind man, you can take off your top garments in his home. When you finish your waiting period, let me know."' (Related by Muslim) Another version of this hadith mentions that the Prophet sent her a word telling her not to get married without letting him know.

This is another case of one of the early companions of the Prophet who migrated with him. It is clear that when she went to the Prophet, she did not have her face covered. The Prophet saw a pretty woman and he gave her a hint about her future marriage. He wanted her as a wife for Usāmah ibn Zayd, the young man who was very dear to him.

2. Cases mentioned in other hadith anthologies:

- Qays ibn Abi Ḥāzim narrated: 'We visited Abu Bakr when he was ill. There was with him a white woman, with painted hands, and she was keeping the flies away from him. She was Asmā' bint 'Umays.' (Related by al-Ṭabarānī)

Asmā' bint 'Umays was one of the early companions of the Prophet. She was married to Jaʿfar ibn Abi Ṭālib and accompanied him on his mission in Abyssinia. Later she was married to Abu Bakr al-Ṣiddīq. After Abu Bakr had passed away, she married ʿAlī ibn Abi Ṭālib.

- Muʿāwiyah narrated: 'I accompanied my father visiting Abu Bakr al-Ṣiddīq. I saw Asmā' [bint 'Umays] standing close to him. She was white. I noticed that Abu Bakr was a white, thin man. He gave me and my father two horses.' (Related by al-Ṭabarānī)

- Zaynab ('Abdullāh ibn Mas'ūd's wife) narrated: 'An old woman used to visit us. She used to do some incantation to cure measles. We had a bed with high legs. When 'Abdullāh came home, he would give some sound [to indicate his arrival]. On one occasion, he came in, and when she heard him, she screened herself. He sat next to me, and he touched me and felt that there was a string. He asked me what was that. I said: It has been used for an incantation to dispel measles from me. He pulled it out, cut it [up] and threw it away. "'Abdullāh's family are in no need of associating partners with God. I heard the Prophet say: 'Incantations, charms, magic and the like are [acts of] polytheism.'" I said: One day I went out and so-and-so saw me. My eye closer to him was tearful. When I said an incantation, it stopped, and if I did not it became tearful again. He said: "That is Satan: when you obey him, he leaves you alone, and when you disobey him, he would place his finger in your eye. Had you followed God's Messenger's example, it would have been better for you and you would be more likely to recover. Wash your eye and pray: 'Lord of mankind, remove this illness. Cure me, for You are the One who cures. There is no cure other than Yours. Make it a cure that takes away all illness.'"' (Related by Ibn Mājah)
- Maymūn ibn Mihrān narrated: 'I visited Umm al-Dardā' and I saw her covering her head with a thick cover, bringing it over her eyebrows.'
- Al-Ḥārith ibn 'Ubayd al-Anṣāri said: 'I saw Umm al-Dardā' going to visit an ill Anṣāri man from the mosque and she was on her mount in an uncovered howdah.' (Related by al-Bukhari in *al-Adab al-Mufrad*)
- Abu Asmā' narrated that he visited Abu Dharr... when he was at al-Rabadhah [a place between Makkah and Madinah]. His wife was with him. She was an ugly black woman wearing

neither colourful clothes nor perfume. He said: 'Do you know what this little one wants me to do? She wants us to go to Iraq. If I go to Iraq, people will tempt me with their worldly things. My dear friend (peace be upon him) told me that next to the bridge leading to Hell there is a slippery way. If we get there with light burden we are more likely to cross it safely than if we are carrying heavy loads.' (Related by Ahmad)

- Abu al-Salīl narrated: 'Abu Dharr's daughter came, wearing two woollen pieces. Her cheeks were reddish black and she had a basket with her. She stood in front of him as he was visited by his friends. She said: "Father, the farmers claimed that these few coins of yours are bad." He said: "Put them down, daughter. All praise be to God; your father owns neither gold nor silver other than these coins."' (Related by Abu Nu'aym)
- Yaḥyā ibn Abi Sulaym narrated: 'I saw Samrā' bint Nuhayk, who had met the Prophet. She was wearing thick robes and a thick head covering, holding a whip with which she punished people. She enjoined what is right and forbade what is wrong.' (Related by al-Ṭabarānī)

Some people may try to discount the evidence in these cases, claiming that these women were mostly elderly and, as such, they were permitted to put aside their veils. We remind these of our earlier comment that these people were the first to seek what is best and bring goodness, and God says in the verse that permits elderly women to put off some of their outer clothes: 'It is better for them to be modest'. Moreover, neither Abu Dharr's daughter nor Samrā' bint Nuhayk were elderly.

Having mentioned all these cases, we may add that these noble female companions of the Prophet: Asmā' bint Abu Bakr, Asmā' bint 'Umays, Zaynab Ibn Mas'ūd's wife, Umm al-Dardā', Subay'ah al-Aslamiyyah and Fāṭimah bint Qays went out with their faces uncovered after the Prophet's wives were ordered to be screened. This is a very clear evidence that women were not required to cover their faces, and that the verse stating the order of the *ḥijāb* did not abrogate its permissibility. Moreover, it was the common practice. Had it been merely permissible and had covering the face been preferable, these pure, chaste and devout women would have opted for what is better.

The general practice of the Prophet's female companions after his wives were ordered to be screened was to leave their faces uncovered

3. From the two *Ṣaḥīḥ* anthologies of al-Bukhari and Muslim:

- Jābir ibn ʿAbdullāh narrated: 'I attended the prayer with God's Messenger on the Eid Day... He went up to the women and admonished them. He said to them: "You, women, donate generously to charity, for you will make up the majority of the dwellers of hell." One of their best, a woman with reddish black cheeks stood up and asked: "Why is it so, Messenger of God?" He answered: "Because you complain too often and you deny your men's kindness." They gave some of their jewellery in charity, throwing in Bilāl's robe whatever they could of their earrings and rings.' (Related by al-Bukhari and Muslim)

This is the case of a woman offering her prayer with the congregation behind God's Messenger (peace be upon him). She listens to the admonition and she is keen to learn more. She asks the Prophet for an explanation of what he said. The Prophet's companion who narrates the hadith describes her as having reddish black cheeks.

- Sahl ibn Saʿd reports that a woman came to the Prophet and said: 'Messenger of God! I have come to make of myself a present to you.' The Prophet looked up and down at her several times, then he lowered his head. When the woman realized that the Prophet did not make a decision concerning her offer, she sat down. One of his companions said: 'Messenger of God, if you have no need of her, give her to me in marriage...' The Prophet said: 'Take her. I marry her to you in return of what you know of the Qur'an.' (Related by al-Bukhari and Muslim)

This is the case of a woman who learnt the Qur'anic verse that says: 'And any believing woman who offers herself freely to the Prophet and whom the Prophet might be willing to wed: [this latter] applies to you alone and not to other believers.' (33: 50) She hoped to be a wife of the Prophet and she offered herself to him in front of other people. The Prophet looked carefully at her and decided not to marry her. One of the Prophet's companions present married her.

- Anas ibn Mālik said to a woman of his family: 'Do you know this woman?' She said: 'Yes.' He said: 'The Prophet passed by her as she was at a grave, weeping. He said to her: "Fear God and remain patient." She said: "Leave me alone. You have not experienced my calamity." He left her and went on. A man passed by her and asked her: "What did God's Messenger say to you?" She said: "I did not recognize him." He said: "He is God's Messenger." She went to his home but did not find a guard at his door. She said: "Messenger of God, I swear by God that I did not recognize you." The Prophet said: "True patience is at the initial shock."' (Related by al-Bukhari)

This is a Muslim woman weeping by the side of a grave, and God's Messenger (peace be upon him) urges her to be patient. Anas sees her and knows her. He mentions her situation to his family. He only recognized her because her face was uncovered.

- 'Aṭā' ibn Rabāḥ narrated: 'Ibn 'Abbās asked me: "Would you like me to show you a woman who will definitely be in heaven?" I said: Yes, indeed. Ibn 'Abbās said: "It is this black woman. She came to the Prophet and said: 'I suffer from epilepsy and I may be exposed when I have a fit. Pray for me.' The Prophet said to her: 'If you wish you bear your affliction with patience and you will be in heaven, or I will pray to God for you to be cured.' She said: 'I will bear it with patience, but pray for me that I may not be exposed during a fit.' He prayed for her."' (Related by al-Bukhari and Muslim) In another version related by al-Bukhari from Ibn Jurayj mentions: "'Aṭā' told me that he saw Umm Zufar, the tall black woman close to the coverings of the Ka'bah.'

The woman in this case has been given the good news of going to heaven. Ibn 'Abbās saw her and knew her. Several years later, Ibn 'Abbās offers to show her to 'Aṭā'. The hadith shows clearly that the woman did not cover her face on the day when she spoke to God's Messenger (peace be upon him) and Ibn 'Abbās got to know her. She must also not have covered her face when Ibn 'Abbās showed her to 'Aṭā' ibn Rabāḥ.

- Abu Hurayrah narrated: 'A man came to the Prophet (peace be upon him). The Prophet sent to his wives, but they replied that they had nothing except water. The Prophet said to those present: "Who will be this man's host?" A man from the Anṣār said he would. He took him home and said to his wife: "Be hospitable to God's Messenger's guest." She said: "We have nothing except my children's dinner." He said: "Prepare your food, put on your light and if your children want their dinner, put them to sleep." She prepared her food, set the light and put her children to sleep. She then went up to the light pretending to set it right, but she put it off. They [i.e. the man and his wife] pretended to the man that they were eating, but in fact they ate nothing. In the morning the Anṣārī man went to God's Messenger (peace be upon him) and the Prophet said: "God smiled at, or liked, what you did last night." God then revealed the verse that says: "They give them preference over themselves, even though they are in want. Those who are saved from their own greed are truly successful." (59: 9)

- Ibn 'Abbās narrated: 'Barīrah's husband was a slave called Mughīth. I can almost see him walking behind her weeping, with his tears wetting his beard. The Prophet said to 'Abbās: "Do you not wonder how Mughīth loves Barīrah and how Barirah hates Mughīth?" The Prophet said to her: "Perhaps you may go back to him." She said: "Messenger of God, are you giving me an order?" He said: "I am only pleading for him." She said: "I have no need of him."' (Related by al-Bukhari and Muslim)

This is the case of a Muslim woman who was a slave and then was set free. She decided to leave her husband who was also a slave. When her husband saw her in the street in Madinah, he wept because he lost her. As she walked in the street without covering her face, Mughīth recognized her. For the same reason, Ibn 'Abbās knew that the woman Mughīth was following was Barīrah.

- Qays ibn Abi Ḥāzim reports: 'Abu Bakr visited a woman from the tribe of Aḥmus called Zaynab bint al-Muhājir, but he found her silent, refusing to speak. He asked about the reason for her silence. He was told that she set out on her hajj pledging to fulfil all duties of pilgrimage without speaking a word. He said to her: "Speak normally. This vow of yours is unlawful because such vows go back to the days of ignorance." She started to speak.' (Related by al-Bukhari)

This is the case of a Muslim woman who made a pledge to perform the hajj without speaking. Abu Bakr visited her and noted that she did not speak. Perhaps she was making signals with her hand. He objected to her action.

ᘓ Zayd ibn Aslam narrated from his father: 'I went to the market place with 'Umar ibn al-Khaṭṭāb. A young lady caught up with him and said: "*Amīr al-Mu'minīn*, my husband has died leaving behind young children..." 'Umar stopped with her, and did not continue walking. He then said: "Welcome to one who is closely related."'

This is the case of a Muslim woman asking the caliph for help. The narrator recognizes that she was young. We imagine that he was aware of this because her face was uncovered.

We conclude these cases that are entered in the two authentic hadith anthologies of al-Bukhari and Muslim with a story that gives clear evidence that the woman involved was not covering her face, and that she was pretty.

ᘓ 'Abdullāh ibn 'Abbās narrated: 'On the Day of Sacrifice, the Prophet (peace be upon him) took al-Faḍl ibn 'Abbās behind him on the back of his she-camel. Al-Faḍl was a handsome man. The Prophet stopped to answer people's questions. A pretty woman from Khath'am came to the Prophet to ask him for a ruling. Al-Faḍl looked at her and admired her beauty. The Prophet turned back as al-Faḍl was looking at her. He put his hand back and held al-Faḍl's chin moving his face away from her. She said: "Messenger of God, the obligation to perform the hajj came at a time when my father is an elderly man who cannot sit up on his camel. Is it sufficient for him that I perform the pilgrimage on his behalf?" The Prophet said: "Yes."' In another version: 'A woman from Khath'am came over. Al-Faḍl kept looking at her and she kept looking at him.' (Related by al-Bukhari and Muslim)

This is the case of a young Muslim woman who was performing the hajj. She was keen to be dutiful to her father, an elderly man.

She went to the Prophet requesting a ruling. Al-Faḍl looked at her admiring her beauty. Another version related by Ahmad mentions that al-Faḍl said: 'I again looked at her, and he turned my face away from hers, doing this three times and I would not desist.' A third version quotes the Prophet saying: 'I saw a young man and a young woman, and I feared Satan for them.'

This is a telling case concerning the uncovering of women's faces. Therefore, we may add here the views of some eminent scholars. Ibn Baṭṭāl, a highly distinguished Hadith scholar who is frequently quoted by Ibn Ḥajar, said: 'This hadith includes an order to lower one's gaze in order not to be exposed to temptation... It also shows that Muslim women are not included in the *ḥijāb* order given to the Prophet's wives. Had it been applicable to all women, the Prophet (peace be upon him) would have ordered the Khath'amī woman to cover herself and he would not have turned al-Faḍl's face away from her... The hadith also serves as evidence confirming that covering women's faces is not obligatory.'

Ibn Ḥazm mentions this hadith and adds: 'Had a woman's face been *'awrah* that should be covered, the Prophet would not have approved that the woman kept her face uncovered in the presence of other people. He would have ordered her to drop some covering over it. Had her face been covered, Ibn 'Abbās would not have distinguished whether she was pretty or ugly.'
In addition to what Ibn Baṭṭal and Ibn Ḥazm said, we may add the following points:

- Had the woman's face been *'awrah* that may not be exposed, particularly if a woman is pretty, God's Messenger (peace be upon him) would have ordered the Khath'amī woman to cover her face with a portion of her cloak, but he did not. This means that a woman's face is not *'awrah* and it is not forbidden to leave it uncovered, even if the woman is very pretty.

- If it is only reprehensible [i.e. *makrūh*] but not forbidden for a pretty woman to keep her face uncovered, the Prophet would have explained this to the Khathʿamī woman, and he would have recommended her to cover her face, but he did not do so. This means that it is not reprehensible for a pretty woman to leave her face uncovered.
- If it is permissible for a pretty woman to uncover her face generally, but it becomes forbidden in the case of casual temptation, the Prophet would have ordered the Khathʿamī woman to cover her face, because the temptation was clear in this case. However, the Prophet did not. Therefore, it is not prohibited for a pretty woman to keep her face uncovered when there is fear of casual temptation, i.e. a few glances.
- If it is only reprehensible [i.e. *makrūh*] but not forbidden for a pretty woman to keep her face uncovered when there is fear of casual temptation, the Prophet would have explained this to the Khathʿamī woman, and he would have recommended her to cover her face, but he did not do so. This means that it is not reprehensible for a pretty woman to leave her face uncovered in a situation where there is casual temptation.

Another incident occurred to al-Faḍl ibn al-ʿAbbās during the hajj season which has some similarity with what he did in the case of the Khathʿamī woman. The Prophet did no more than turn al-Faḍl's face the other way:

- Jābir ibn ʿAbdullāh narrated: 'God's Messenger (peace be upon him) stayed nine years without offering the hajj. In the tenth year, he announced to people that God's Messenger would be performing the hajj. Large numbers of people arrived in Madinah, all of them eager to join God's Messenger (peace be upon him) and follow his practice. We set out with him...

He then mounted al-Qaṣwā', up to al-Mash'ar al-Ḥarām. He faced the *qiblah*, supplicated, glorified God and declared His oneness. He remained there until it was very clear light, but moved on before sunrise.

He took behind him al-Faḍl ibn 'Abbās who was a white, smart young man with fine hair. When God's Messenger moved on, some women passed by him, moving fast. Al-Faḍl looked at them, and God's Messenger put his hand on al-Faḍl's face, but al-Faḍl turned the other way to look at them. The Prophet also moved his hand the other side and put it on al-Faḍl's face, to stop him looking.' (Related by Muslim)

4. Cases reported in other hadith anthologies. These took place after the *ḥijāb* order.

   - Abu Kabshah al-Anṣārī said: 'God's Messenger (peace be upon him) was sitting with his companions. He went into his home and came back, having taken a bath. We said: "Messenger of God, has something happened?" He said: "Yes. A woman passed by and I felt the urge for a woman. I went to one of my wives and I had her. This is what you should do. Your best action is to do what is legitimate." (Related by Ahmad)
   - Ibn Abi Ḥusayn narrated: 'Durrah bint Abu Lahab was married to al-Ḥārith ibn 'Abdullāh ibn Nawfal, and she gave him his three sons: 'Uqbah, al-Walīd and Abu Muslim. She then migrated to Madinah, and people taunted her about her father. She went to God's Messenger and said: "Messenger of God, am I the only one born to unbelievers?" He said: "What has happened?" She said: "The people of Madinah hurt me about my parents." The Prophet said to her: "When you come to the Ẓuhr Prayer, take a position where I can see you." The Prophet (peace be upon him) led the Ẓuhr Prayer then turned towards the people and said: "People, do you all

have ancestors and I have none?" 'Umar ibn al-Khaṭṭāb rose quickly and said to him: "May God displease anyone who caused your displeasure." The Prophet said: "This one is the daughter of my uncle. Let no one say to her anything other than good."' (Related by al-Ṭabarānī)

The relevance in this story is that people recognized her because she went about with her face uncovered. They said whatever they said about her father who was the Prophet's uncle but a determined unbeliever. He is condemned in the Qur'an. His daughter was taunted about this and she complained to the Prophet. The Prophet wanted her to be in a visible place when she prayed so that people would know her when the Prophet confirmed her relationship with him. He pointed to her and said that she was his cousin. Had she been covering her face, they would not have known her and the admonition would have had no effect.

- A man from the Hudhayl tribe said: 'I saw 'Abdullāh ibn 'Amr ibn al-'Āṣ. His home was in the Ḥil area while his praying place was in the Ḥaram. As I was at his place he saw Umm Sa'īd bint Abu Jahl carrying a bow and walking like men. 'Abdullāh said: "Who is this?" I said: "Umm Sa'īd bint Abu Jahl." He said: "I heard God's Messenger say: 'A man who emulates women and a woman who emulates men do not belong to us.'"'

Evidence 3: This is based on texts mentioning that some women covered their faces

The texts that we shall mention now stating that women covered their faces with a veil or something similar imply that such face covering was infrequently or rarely used. This is the reason for the narrator to mention it. Had face coverings been women's normal practice, or had all women been covering their faces, the narrator would not have mentioned it.

We will not include in this respect any text referring to the Mothers of the Believers, the Prophet's wives, because they were the ones required to remain behind a screen when at home and to cover their faces when they went out.

It is especially significant that the word *niqab*, i.e. veil, or its derivatives, was only used once by the Prophet in the hadiths included in the two *Ṣaḥīḥ* anthologies of al-Bukhari and Muslim, and also in other anthologies of authentic hadiths. On this single occasion, the Prophet did not encourage wearing a veil. In fact, it was mentioned so as to indicate that its wearing was forbidden to a woman who is in a state of consecration.

The other texts that mention the *niqab* and its derivatives are drawn from hadith anthologies other than the two *Ṣaḥīḥ* ones. Some of their chains of transmission are lacking in authenticity, such as the case related by Abu Dāwūd and narrated by Qays ibn Shammās. Others cannot be determined with regard to authenticity. We are including these as mere historical evidence. The clear ruling that wearing a veil was practised by some Muslim women and approved by the Prophet (peace be upon him) is evidenced by the following hadith entered in al-Bukhari's *Ṣaḥīḥ*:

> ‘Abdullāh ibn ‘Umar narrated: ‘A man stood up and said: "Messenger of God, what clothes do you order us to wear during consecration?" The Prophet said: "Do not wear robes, trousers, turbans or cloaks with hoods. A man who does not have slippers may wear shoes but he should cut them below the ankles. Do not wear anything that has been perfumed with saffron or *warss*. A woman who is in a state of consecration must not wear a veil or gloves."' (Related by al-Bukhari)

Most Fiqh scholars explain that the hadith states that the man's consecration applies to his head and the woman's applies to her face.

Therefore, a man in consecration must keep his head uncovered and a woman in consecration must keep her face uncovered. We should also remember that a man wears a turban as an adornment on his head, not to cover any part of his *'awrah*. The veil serves the same purpose for a woman: it is an adornment on her face and covers no *'awrah*. It does not fit that *'awrah* is kept covered in ordinary situations and then uncovered in a situation of *iḥrām*, or consecration; this, whether we are speaking of the *'awrah* of a man or a woman.

The following reports are from hadith anthologies other than the two *Ṣaḥīḥs:*

- 'Abdullāh ibn al-Zubayr narrated: 'At the time when Makkah fell to Islam, Hind bint 'Utbah and other women embraced Islam and they came to God's Messenger (peace be upon him) when he was at al-Abṭaḥ [An open area in Makkah.] Hind said: "Messenger of God, all praise be to God who has given supremacy to the faith He has chosen. My relation to you will certainly benefit me. Muhammad, I am a woman who believes in God and His Messenger." She then removed her veil and said: "I am Hind bint 'Utbah." God's Messenger said: "You are welcome."' (Related by Ibn Sa'd in *al-Ṭabaqāt*)
- 'Āṣim al-Aḥwal narrated: 'We used to visit Ḥafṣah bint Sīrīn and she would place her cloak in this way, using it as a veil. We would say to her: May God bestow mercy on you. God says: "Such elderly women as are past the prospect of marriage incur no sin if they lay aside their [outer] garments, provided they do not make a showy display of their charms." (24: 60) She would say: "What does God say next?" We continue [the verse] saying: "But it is better for them to be modest." She would say: "This confirms the cloak."' (Related by al-Bayhaqi)
- Al-Bukhari includes the following report with an incomplete chain of transmission, without mentioning the narrator he

heard it from: "Samurah ibn Jundab accepted the testimony of a woman who was wearing a veil."

- Qays ibn Shammās narrated: 'A woman called Umm Khallād came to the Prophet wearing a *niqab* and asking information about her son who was killed. Some of the Prophet's companions said to her: "Have you come to ask about your son and you are wearing a veil?" She said: "I may have the calamity of losing my son, but I shall not lose my modesty." God's Messenger said to her: "Your son shall have the reward of two martyrs." She asked: "Why is it so, Messenger of God?" He said: 'Because he was killed by people who follow earlier revelations." (Related by Abu Dāwūd)

Evidence 4: Derived from texts describing a woman as white, black, pretty, etc. and the keen interest of commentators to find out the names of the women referred to in these texts.

Had covering women's faces been a common practice, it would definitely have led to withholding the identity of the Muslim woman and overlooked her most distinctive feature. Indeed, the Prophet's companions would not have mentioned women's names or described them. Nor would scholars who wrote commentaries and interpretations of hadiths have carefully researched the identity and names of women mentioned in hadiths. They would certainly have not mentioned their physical features. Here are some examples of such descriptions:

- Ibn 'Abbās narrated: '... A pretty woman from Khath'am came over.'
- 'Aṭā' ibn Rabāḥ narrated: 'Ibn 'Abbās asked me: "Would you like me to show you a woman who will definitely be in heaven?" I said: Yes, indeed. Ibn 'Abbās said: "It is this black woman."'
- Jābir ibn 'Abdullāh narrated: '... One of their best, a woman with reddish black cheeks stood up and asked.'

- Qays ibn Abi Ḥāzim narrated: 'We visited Abu Bakr when he was ill. There was with him a white woman, with painted hands...'
- Abu Asmā' narrated that he visited Abu Dharr... when he was at al-Rabadhah. His wife was with him. She was an ugly black woman wearing neither colourful clothes nor perfume...'
- Abu al-Salīl narrated: 'Abu Dharr's daughter came, wearing two woollen pieces. Her cheeks were reddish black...'

And here are some examples of verifying women's names:

- Ibn 'Abbās narrated: '... Only one woman said: "Yes." She was the only one to answer him. Ḥasan [one of the narrators] does not know who she was.' Ibn Ḥajar said: 'I could not ascertain the name of this woman but something in my mind tells me that she was Asmā' bint Yazīd ibn al-Sakan.'
- Anas narrated: 'The Prophet (peace be upon him) passed by a woman as she was close to a grave, weeping...'Ibn Ḥajar said: 'I could not ascertain her name.'
- Abu Sa'īd al-Khudrī narrated: '... A woman said: "How about two?" He said: "And two."' Ibn Ḥajar said: 'The woman referred to here is Umm Sulaym, but some mention someone else.'
- Anas narrated: 'A woman came to God's Messenger (peace be upon him) offering herself to him...' Ibn Ḥajar said: 'I could not find out who she was'.
- Asmā' said that a woman said: 'Messenger of God, my husband has another wife. Do I do wrong if I say that my husband has given me things which he has not?' Ibn Ḥajar said: 'I could not find out who this woman was or her husband's name.'

Evidence 5: This evidence is based on the meaning of texts related to women's participation in social life

The practice of covering a woman's face so that it is not seen by men and to prevent temptation makes a woman shy off meeting men. Therefore, she is keen to stay away from men's society, even though the meeting would be honourable and free of whatever is unbecoming. It also gives men a feeling of reluctance to meet women. With such feelings, a sort of isolation develops between men and women, which only increases as time goes on. Furthermore, people claim that moral standards have deteriorated and this is added to the claim of 'preventing temptation' which normally accompanies the trend of extra covering. With such increased isolation, if necessity requires that men and women meet, such an unusual meeting will bring about a shock and make both aware of the mutual temptation between them. In turn, this strengthens the need to keep the two sexes apart within Muslim society, so as not to cause embarrassment and to prevent any such temptation. Thus, society reasserts the practice of women's isolation, deprives them of taking part in social life and makes meetings between men and women a rarity. All this results from the practice of covering women's faces.

Hence, we say that covering women's faces is very often,[5] if not always, linked to women's isolation and the avoidance of meeting men. Likewise, uncovering women's faces leads to women's full participation and to meeting with men. Face covering becomes indicative of women's isolation and isolation indicates face covering. In reverse, women's participation in social activity alongside men and face uncovering are mutually indicative of each other. The general characteristic of the Muslim society during the Prophet's lifetime was that women met men and participated in all areas and activities, without there being any case of emergency or pressing need. Their meeting together was often unintended, happening only as life required, and perhaps to achieve some

5. We say very often because an exception should be made in the case of some bedouin societies when women need to work, almost daily, outside the home. Such women may have a lighter version of covering their faces which enables them to move and work easily, and they remain easily identifiable within their compact society.

gain that improved life. In Chapter 4 of Volume 2 of this series we noted that during the Prophet's lifetime, women met men in social visits, as guests and hosts, in exchanges of gifts, enquiring after patients, doing some good actions, in marking occasions, at mealtimes, as well as in the mosque, on military expeditions and during professional, social and political activities. Is it not true to say that all these aspects of participation and meeting indicate that the predominant case during the Prophet's lifetime was that women did not cover their faces?

Four: Scholars' statements indicating face exposure

1. In *al-Muwaṭṭa'* we read: 'Mālik was asked whether greeting women is appropriate. He said: "I do not dislike this in the case of an elderly woman, but I do not like it in the case of a young one." Mālik's answer indicates that women mostly uncovered their faces. Otherwise, how can a person distinguish an elderly woman from a younger one?'
2. Ibn Ḥajar writes in *Fatḥ al-Bārī*: 'Al-Mutawalli, a leading Shāfi'ī scholar, said: "If the woman is pretty and one fears temptation, a greeting is not appropriate, neither to begin with nor to respond to. If either one offers the greeting, the other is discouraged from replying. If the woman is elderly and there is no chance of temptation, greeting is permissible." The difference between this view and that of the Mālikī scholars is the details given in the case of a younger woman and whether she is pretty or not. Beauty invites temptation, which is not the case in all younger women.' Again, this statement by al-Mutawallī indicates that women's faces were mostly uncovered. Otherwise, how could one distinguish a pretty young woman from a plain one?
3. In *Fatḥ al-Bārī* we read: 'Women pray with men at the time of eclipse.' Stating this chapter heading, al-Bukhari means to refute the view of those who do not approve and require women to offer the eclipse prayer individually. This view is reported to

have been expressed by al-Thawrī and some Kūfī scholars. In *al-Mudawwanah*: 'Women pray at home, but elderly ones come out.' Al-Shāfi'ī said: 'All should come out except the one who is very pretty.'

This last statement by al-Shāfi'ī indicates that women mostly kept their faces uncovered. Otherwise what difference could be there between one whose beauty is of the average type and one who is very beautiful, if they are all covering their faces?

4. Al-Nawawī, a highly distinguished Shāfi'ī scholar, said: 'The view of our school, as well as the schools of Mālik and Ahmad, and also the majority of scholars, is that it is not necessary that the man intending to make an offer of marriage should first obtain her consent in order to look at her. He may do this when she is unaware and without prior information... The Prophet gave this permission without making any qualification and did not stipulate her agreement. She is likely to be too shy to give such permission. Moreover, seeking such permission may have unwelcome consequences. The man may see the woman and decide not to pursue his interest in her. She may thus feel hurt. Therefore, our scholars say that it is desirable that he sees her before making a proposal of marriage, so that if he decides not to go ahead, he does not hurt her.'

That Fiqh scholars say that it is desirable to look at the woman to whom one is thinking of making a marriage offer when she is unaware means that in most cases Muslim women do not cover their faces outside their homes. Had she covered her face, the man would not be able to look at her unless he cast a stealthy look at her when she was at home. If he did this, he might see more than her face and hands, which is not permissible according to Shāfi'ī and other scholars.

5. ‘Alī al-Marghīnānī, a distinguished Ḥanafī scholar said: ‘The entire body of a free woman is *‘awrah*, apart from her face and hands. This is based on the Prophet’s hadith: “The woman is a covered *‘awrah*.” These two parts are excepted so that their exposure serves as a test. That Ḥanafī scholars say that the exposure serves as a test means that the test is applicable to Muslim women generally, not merely to a minority of them.

CHAPTER IV

Further evidence endorsing face uncovering

Foreword: The difficulty of citing evidence for the permissible

Duties and prohibitions are limited, and texts concerning them are also numbered. Every duty or prohibition is stated in a clear text. What is permissible is unlimited. It is not possible for the limited to encompass the unlimited. Hence, Fiqh scholars state: 'Everything is initially permissible unless a prohibition is stated by the Legislator.'

When the Prophet was asked about what a person may wear when he is in a state of consecration, his answer did not enumerate what is permissible to wear, because it is unlimited. He simply stated what may not be worn because it is limited: 'Abdullāh ibn 'Umar narrated: 'A man stood up and said: "Messenger of God, what clothes do you order us to wear during consecration?" The Prophet said: "Do not wear robes, trousers, turbans or cloaks with hoods. A man who does not have slippers may wear shoes but he should cut them below the ankles. Do not wear anything that has been perfumed with saffron or *warss*. A woman who is in a state of consecration must not wear a veil or gloves."' (Related by al-Bukhari)

We need only to consider that when the Prophet's wives were ordered to have a screen, the order was given in clear terms: 'When you ask the Prophet's wives for something, do so from behind a screen.' (33: 53) What was permissible to them before this order is not stated in any text. The evidence that the Prophet's wives left their faces uncovered before this order occurs within explaining a particular situation, as one of the Prophet's wives needed to mention how a man who was unrelated to her recognized her. We mentioned this in the previous chapter, but it is useful to remind ourselves of it: 'Ṣafwān ibn al-Mu'aṭṭal al-Sulamī al-Dhakwānī was left behind the army. He started moving early at night and reached the place where I was in the morning. He could see the black shape of a sleeping person. He came over to me and recognized me. He used to see me before we were ordered to be screened.' (Related by al-Bukhari and Muslim)

We do not have any text concerning the permissibility of the *niqab* which some women used to wear before and after Islam. However, at the time of the Farewell Pilgrimage, an outline of what is not permissible during consecration was given and we learnt that a woman in consecration is forbidden to cover her face. The fact that this prohibition has been clearly stated means that a woman may wear a *niqab* or veil when she is not in consecration.

The same applies to the permissibility of women leaving their faces uncovered. There was no text to specify this, but when there was a contravention of what Islam requires, a text was provided to outline what is prohibited. The prohibition defined what is permissible to expose: 'Ā'ishah narrated that Asmā' bint Abu Bakr entered God's Messenger's home wearing thin clothes. The Prophet turned away from her and said to her: 'Asmā', when a woman has attained puberty, it is not permissible for any part of her body to be seen, except this and this, pointing to his face and hands.' (Related by Abu Dāwūd)

When scholars speak about the permissibility of leaving women's faces uncovered, they do so within the context of explaining what is obligatory, permissible, discouraged or prohibited. When they state that a woman must cover her *'awrah* when praying, they explain that all her body is *'awrah* except her face and hands. When they discuss the duty or desirability that a man intending marriage should see the woman he intends to marry, they state that he may look at her face, because it is not part of her *'awrah*. When they mention when a woman in mourning should avoid, they include the *niqab* in that list, which indicates that uncovering her face is perfectly permissible. They also mention that wearing a veil in prayer is reprehensible, which means that leaving her face uncovered is perfectly permissible.

Within the context of the difficulty of providing evidence confirming the permissibility of uncovering women's faces, we are reminded of Ibn Taymiyyah's valid argument about the permissibility of female slaves uncovering their heads in order to be distinguished from free women. He said: 'There is nothing in the Sunnah to confirm that slave women need not cover their heads or that they may show their adornments. However, the Qur'an does not order them as it orders free women. The Sunnah showed in practice, not in a general text, that they are to be distinguished from free women. It was the common practice of believers that free women covered themselves, but not slave women.'

We say in the same way that there is no text in the Qur'an or the Sunnah telling free women not to cover their faces or to show their adornments. There is only a hadith, graded as *mursal* [i.e. with an incomplete chain of transmission], but strengthened in other ways, which says: 'When a woman has attained puberty, it is not permissible that any part of her body be seen, except this and this, pointing to his face and hands.' (Related by Abu Dāwūd) However, the Qur'an does not command Muslim women as it commands the Prophet's wives: 'Do so from behind a screen'. After this *ḥijāb* order, the Sunnah distinguished them in practice from other Muslim women. As for action by the Prophet's wives, 'Ā'ishah narrated: 'Ṣafwān ibn al-Mu'aṭṭal was left behind the army. He started moving early at night and reached the place where I was in the morning. He could see the black shape of a sleeping person... I woke up as he said *innā lillāh wa innā ilayhi rāji'ūn* as he recognized me... I covered my face with my cloak...'. (Related by al-Bukhari and Muslim) As for the general practice of Muslim women, Jābir reports that God's Messenger (peace be upon him) saw a woman, and he went to his wife Zaynab and had with her whatever he wanted. He then came out and said to his companions: '... If any of you sees a woman, he should go to his wife. That will clear what he experiences.' In another version, Jābir said that he heard the Prophet say: 'If any of you sees a woman and is attracted by her, he should go to his wife and have intercourse with her. That is enough to remove what he has experienced.' (Related by Muslim)

In the same vein, Subay'ah bint al-Ḥārith, a companion of the Prophet, reports that she was married to Sa'd ibn Khawlah, but he died during the Prophet's pilgrimage. Only a short while after that she gave birth to her child. When she regained her strength, she started to wear make-up expecting a proposal. (In the version related by Ahmad: she wore kohl, henna and put on a good appearance.) Abu al-San'bil ibn Ba'kak came to her and said: 'How come you are adorned expecting a proposal, hoping to get married?'

We also have the hadith in which Ibn 'Abbās said to 'Aṭā': 'Would you like me to show you a woman who will definitely be in heaven? ... It is this black woman. She came to the Prophet and said: I suffer from epilepsy and I may be exposed when I have a fit. Pray for me. The Prophet said to her: 'If you wish you bear your affliction with patience and you will be in heaven, or I will pray to God for you to be cured.' She said: 'I will bear it with patience, but pray for me that I may not be exposed during a fit.' He prayed for her.' (Related by al-Bukhari and Muslim) Another version, related by al-Bukhari from Ibn Jurayj, mentions: 'Aṭā' told me that he saw Umm Zufar, the tall black woman close to the coverings of the Ka'bah.

We see that the Sunnah does not include a general statement to distinguish the Prophet's wives from other Muslim women. It was the practice in Muslim society that the Prophet's wives remained behind a screen, but when they went out, they covered their faces. Other Muslim women went out with their faces uncovered.

Finally, we may say that a person may do or leave what is permissible, as one pleases. No one is to blame for what one does or leaves out. The permissible is available to all, without comment from anyone, either in encouragement or in warning. God's Messenger tells the truth: 'The permissible is that which God has made permissible in His Book, and the forbidden is that which He forbids in His Book. What is not mentioned is left open.' (Related by al-Tirmidhī)

We conclude this chapter's introductory paragraphs by saying that there is plenty of secondary evidence indicating that Islam makes it permissible for women to leave their faces uncovered. As for the detailed evidence, this is as follows:

Secondary evidence 1: No clear statement in the Qur'an or the Sunnah requires covering the woman's face

The fact that there is no text that speaks about leaving the woman's face uncovered means that it is permissible, because neither the Qur'an nor the Sunnah includes any text that requires the woman to cover her face. We note that all obligations stated in the Qur'an are explained in detail in the Sunnah, with hadiths providing details of the way they should be implemented. The hadiths also urge their observation and denounce ignoring or neglecting them. Do we find in the Qur'an a clear statement regarding an obligation to cover women's faces, or do we find in the hadiths a proper explanation of it?

It goes without saying that if the Qur'an states an obligation that confirms what is common practice, the need for clarification in hadiths is minimal. By contrast, if the Qur'anic obligation runs contrary to what is commonly practised, there will be great need for clarifying hadiths. Such need also increases in a situation where a contrary practice prevails and also when the obligation is particularly important. To my way of thinking, I consider that covering the woman's face is very important because it concerns all people and applies to all Muslim women. How did women appear before the revelation of the verses speaking about their attire and adornments? Did they cover or uncover their faces in most situations? If the common practice was to cover women's faces and the Qur'an made this obligatory, the need for clarification would be minimal. By contrast, if the common practice was to uncover women's faces and the Qur'an required them to cover, clarification would be greatly needed. We know, on the basis of clear evidence, that the common practice of women in Makkah and Madinah was to leave their faces uncovered. The evidence is what 'Ā'ishah said: 'He used to see me before we were ordered to be screened'. Had the Qur'anic verses stated that women must cover their faces, we would have had hadiths to stress this requirement and deter a woman from leaving her face uncovered, but there is nothing of the sort. The Qur'anic verses allow more than one interpretation, but the hadiths do not include anything that implies that covering women's faces is a duty.

Imam al-Ḥaramayn al-Juwaynī states a clear principle of Islamic law: 'What is unknown of prohibition, through a categorical statement, remains permissible. The reason is that no ruling applies to people unless it is based on clear evidence. If there is no evidence of prohibition, a prohibitive ruling becomes impossible'. He also said:

'To stick to what is probable where a definitive is needed is not a quality of scholars of good standing'.

Secondary evidence 2: Had covering the face truly been a duty, it would have been widely practised and become an aspect of religion that is essentially known. It would be something that is applicable to all and known to both the general public and society's elite.

Citing different cases where a clear order, which would have become widely-known, would have been given to indicate a duty, Imam ibn Taymiyyah said: 'Had the removal of the traces of semen from the body and clothes been obligatory, it could not have been left unstated by the Prophet, as this is something that applies to all. Likewise, had the *wudu*, i.e. ablution, been a duty, an order confirming that would have been necessary. Had the Prophet ordered it, it would have been widely transmitted by Muslims, because its transmission would have been necessary'. He said elsewhere: 'Had covering the hands during prayer been a duty, the Prophet would have explained it. The same applies to the feet'.

Justice Ibn Rushd said that a verdict on something that is commonly or universally applicable should be transmitted as *mutawātir*, or close to it.

If such matters are included in the 'commonly applicable' and their rulings need to be widely known, the issue of covering women's faces is definitely more so. In other words, had covering women's faces been a duty, and it is something that applies to all Muslim women, there would be cause for reporting it and many reports would have mentioned it. There would be many hadiths reporting it and these would be transmitted in the *mutawātir* way, or close to it.

Had it been so, there would be no different views about it. In fact, such a matter would not only be widely reported but would have been the common practice of Muslim women, developing into a social phenomenon that is visible to all. However, the situation in this case is the opposite, indicated by the different views concerning the meanings of the relevant verses stating: 'Tell believing women... not to display their charms except what may ordinarily appear thereof,' (24: 31) and 'They should draw over themselves some of their outer garments.' (33: 59) Some explain these as meaning that the woman's face should be covered and others say it remains uncovered, as we have explained in Chapter 2. This certainly suggests that there is no obligation. Had it been obligatory, it would have been known to all Muslims, as it is applicable to all. In other words, the very difference is itself evidence that it is permissible to leave women's faces uncovered.

We may attribute the reports that require covering women's faces to a number of factors, such as:

a. The screening of the Prophet's wives. Some scholars might not have understood that it was applicable to them only, and hence they tended to apply it to all women. We will be discussing the fact that the *ḥijāb* applies specifically to the Prophet's wives in Chapter 2 of Volume 5.
b. That some women used to wear the *niqab* during the Prophet's lifetime. This might have led some scholars to say that covering the face was obligatory or desirable.
c. That different groups of people came to Madinah after the spread of Islam into large areas. This might have increased the number of women wearing the *niqab* to avoid the gaze of such strangers. This might have led some to say that covering the face is a duty to prevent temptation.
d. Confusing the permissible with the obligatory in some cases. It happens that some devout people urge doing what is permissible and this leads to an increase in the number of people who do it. As time passes, some people might be

under the impression that it is a duty, the negligence of which incurs a sin. I think this applies to the case of covering women's faces. We note that scholars of methodology warn against such confusion. They advise that a scholar should refrain from doing the permissible on some occasions so that people do not get the impression that it is obligatory.

Imam al-Ghazālī says some precious words about what the Prophet delivered through ensuring its wide circulation, and this would confirm that a duty to cover women's faces, if true, is something that should essentially be known to all people. Imam al-Ghazālī says:

> A report by a single person is acceptable if it relates to something that is widely applicable... Whatever is reported by a person of known integrity must be believed if it is possible that he is telling the truth. This is different from a single person's report of something that common practice makes impossible not to be widely known, such as a case of assassinating a governor in the market place, or the sacking of a minister, or an event taking place in the mosque and preventing people from offering Friday Prayer... All such matters invite publicity and are impossible to suppress....
>
> A question may be asked: what is the criterion that defines what the Prophet delivered through ensuring its wide circulation. We say in answer that there is no such criterion that confirms its logical happening. God does whatever He wishes in how He assigns tasks to His Messenger. However, the Prophet's actions tell us that this has happened. When we look at what is transmitted through word of mouth, we realize that it is of four types. The first is the Qur'an and we know that the Prophet was keen to make it widely circulated.

> The second type covers the five pillars of Islam, and the Prophet made this known to all people. The third concerns the fundamentals of unessential transactions such as sales and marriages. Again, such information has been widely transmitted. Indeed, other transactions such as divorce, setting slaves free and allowing slaves to buy their freedom are widely known among scholars and are absolutely defined, either through *mutawātir* reporting or being reported by single people in the presence of a large number of people without any making an objection. The fourth covers the details of these pillars, such as what invalidates prayer, acts of worship or purification, etc. Such details include some that are widely reported and others reported by single reporters.

Al-Ghazālī's words give us the following conclusion: a matter that common practice makes impossible not to be widely known will certainly be publicized and cannot be suppressed. As the five pillars of Islam have been circulated so as to be known to all people, and the fundamentals of unessential transactions are widely known among scholars, we say that the definition of the woman's *'awrah* and whether her face is part of her *'awrah* or not must be similarly known. The point is that a Muslim woman's life cannot be set right unless she is fully aware of it and she implements it when she goes out, as well as in every situation where she finds herself with men. It is indeed a matter of religion that must, essentially, be known to all people, during the Prophet's lifetime and during the early generations of Muslims and later ones. The great majority of early scholars, perhaps with the exception of one or a handful, agree that the woman's *'awrah* is all her body except her face and hands. This is almost unanimously agreed upon by those scholars. Therefore, we say with certainty that what is acceptable in the matter of the *'awrah* is what is agreed upon by the majority of scholars, and that the odd views are discarded, particularly in such a matter that must, essentially, be known to all.

Secondary evidence 3: Leaving the woman's face uncovered is the normal practice in human life

Women in all ages did not cover their faces, since this is the normal practice that human nature requires. This was the practice of prophets (peace be upon them all). The Prophet said: 'Abraham migrated with Sarah and they entered the city of a certain king... People said: "Abraham came with a woman who is most beautiful."' (Related by al-Bukhari and Muslim)

Thus was the case with the followers of the prophets, or rather those of their followers who continued to follow the teachings of their prophets. Women who followed divine religions, in the East and the West, continued to wear long, all-body covering clothing with head veils for many centuries. Christian nuns continued to adhere to this dress code even after Christian women shed their modesty with the advent of modern civilization. The same practice was part of what remained among the Arabs of the religion taught by Abraham and Ishmael. Women generally wore long robes and head coverings all the time. Some women, definitely not all, used to wear the *niqab* but they would take it off on occasions, particularly in difficult times.

With the advent of Islam, a head cover, not a veil or *niqab*, was the normal practice of God-fearing Muslim women in Makkah and later in Madinah:

- Al-Ḥārith ibn al-Ḥārith al-Ghāmidī narrated: 'I said to my father when we were at Mina: "What are these people?" He said: "They are a group surrounding one of their own people who has changed his religion." We went over and saw God's Messenger (peace be upon him) calling on people to believe in God's oneness while they rejected what he said and kept abusing him until it was midday when people dispersed. A woman came over, weeping, with her neck visible. She was carrying a jug of water and a handkerchief. He took it from her, drank some and performed the ablution. He then lifted his head to her and said: "Daughter, cover your neck and do not fear for your father being overcome or humiliated." I asked who the woman was and people said: "She is Zaynab, his daughter."'

- Anas narrated: 'During the Battle of Uhud people deserted the Prophet (peace be upon him)... I saw 'Ā'ishah bint Abu Bakr and Umm Sulaym. Both lifted their skirts and I could see their anklets. They quickly jerked waterskins on their backs and poured the water in people's mouths.'
- 'Aṭā' ibn Rabāḥ narrated: 'Ibn 'Abbās asked me: "Would you like me to show you a woman who will definitely be in heaven?" I said: Yes, indeed. Ibn 'Abbās said: "It is this black woman."'

Moreover, the Prophet's wives used to leave their faces uncovered until a special order was given to them in particular that they should be screened. Only after this order, did they cover their faces when they went out. We mentioned earlier how Ṣafwān ibn al-Mu'aṭṭal recognized 'Ā'ishah because he used to see her before this order, and how she covered her face with the end of her cloak.

Secondary evidence 4: Life needs require that women uncover their faces

1. Uncovering faces helps recognizing and identifying one's interlocutor:
   Al-Qaffāl said: 'The order to Muslim women "not to reveal their charms except what may ordinarily appear thereof," refers to what a person reveals in normal practice. For women, this refers to the face and hands... They are ordered to cover what there is no need to uncover, while they were permitted to expose what is normally exposed and what there is need to reveal. This is an aspect of the easy nature of Islamic law. Since the uncovering

of women's faces and hands is almost necessary, scholars are in general agreement that they are not part of the woman's *'awrah*'.

One of the Fiqh rules mentioned by scholars says: 'Needs are treated in the same way as necessities.'

Ibn Qudāmah said: 'It is reported that the Prophet (peace be upon him) said: "A woman is *'awrah*." (Related by al-Tirmidhī) This applies to all her body except her face, because its exposure is needed. The rest remains so.'

We may ask: Was there a special need during the time of Ibn Qudāmah (541-620 AH, 1147-1223 CE) and it does not apply to our own time, or is it a universal human need that applies in all times and to all communities? Scholars clearly state that it is permissible to look at a woman's face when some business is being done. In his voluminous work, *al-Mughnī*, Ibn Qudāmah, who was a highly distinguished Ḥanbalī scholar, says: 'A witness may look at the woman who is the subject of his testimony so as to be certain that the testimony applies to her. Ahmad said: 'A witness may not testify against a woman unless he has known her in person. If a person has a transaction of sale or rent, he should look at her face so that he knows her and could come back to her in case of some disagreement... It is reported that Ahmad discouraged this if one is dealing with a young woman, but did not discourage it if she is elderly. Perhaps his discouragement applies to one who fears temptation or may decide not to go ahead with the transaction. In the case of need and absence of temptation, there is no problem'.

I may add here that testimony may be required for something that occurred at a previous time and the woman did not deliberately uncover her face in anticipation of a need for testimony. How can testimony then be given unless the woman's face is always uncovered?

In his book *al-Majmūʿ*, al-Nawawī, a distinguished Shāfiʿī scholar, says: 'It is permissible for each of them, i.e. the man and the woman, to look at each other's faces when they are conducting a business transaction, because they will need that to demand their rights under the contract and to return what needs to be returned. This is also permissible when giving testimony, because of the need to know the woman when witnessing the transaction and testifying for it.' He also says: 'There is need to show the woman's face when buying and selling, and to show her hand in giving and taking. Therefore, these organs are not considered as part of the *ʿawrah*.'

Needless to say, people need to know each other in countless forms of transactions, not only in sales, rents and testimonies. Indeed, they may need to know more than the physical appearance of a person, such as age, even approximately, colour such as being white, dark or black, normal facial expression such as being cheerful or tending to be gloomy. Many feelings and inner thoughts may be reflected in one's face, such as delight or sorrow, pleasure or anger, determination or despair, etc. People may need to know any or all of these matters when they deal with one another, according to the nature and circumstances of their dealing, so that each one will understand the other(s). This type of mutual knowledge and understanding serves some interest in a certain degree, and such interests may be of essential, needful or complementary types.

2. Keeping faces uncovered helps to maintain bonds between relatives
   Thus a young man will get to know the daughters of his paternal and maternal uncles and aunts, and a young woman will get to

know the sons of her paternal and maternal uncles and aunts. Both will also know the spouses of their uncles and aunts, paternal and maternal. Further a man will get to know his wife's sisters and a woman will know her husband's brothers. If, in contrast, we take a situation where women's faces are generally covered, and consequently this leads women to stay away from all men other than those whom they cannot marry, i.e. siblings, uncles and nephews, how will ties of kinship be maintained and strengthened, as Islam requires? How will they visit each other when they fall sick? How will they bid each other farewell when they travel, or welcome them when they return? Will a man go to the home of his married cousin and sit with her husband to have a pleasant conversation and exchange kind feelings, without seeing his cousin for whose sake the visit is paid? Is this what God has ordered? With regard to Muslim women generally, God says: 'They must not display their charms to any but their husbands, or their fathers, or their husbands' fathers, or their sons, or their husbands' sons, or their brothers, or their brothers' sons, or their sisters' sons, or their womenfolk...' (24: 31). He did not say that they must be screened from all men other than these. The screening or *ḥijāb* order applies only to the Prophet's wives.

Here are some examples of how the Prophet maintained ties with his own kinswomen:

- 'Ā'ishah said: 'God's Messenger (peace be upon him) visited Ḍubāʿah bint al-Zubayr ibn 'Abd al-Muṭṭalib. He said to her: "Do you want to perform the hajj?" She said: "By God, I am often ill." He said: "Then go for hajj and make a condition. You say: 'My Lord, my place of release [from consecration] is wherever You detain me.'" She was married to al-Miqdād ibn al-Aswad.' (Related by al-Bukhari and Muslim) Ḍubāʿah was the Prophet's cousin as her father was al-Zubayr, the Prophet's uncle.

- Umm Hāni' narrated: 'On the day of the takeover of Makkah, Fāṭimah sat to the left of God's Messenger (peace be upon him) and Umm Hāni' to his right. The maid brought a jug full of a drink. She gave it to him. He drank and gave it to Umm Hāni' and she drank...' (Related by al-Ḥākim) Umm Hāni' was the Prophet's cousin as her father was his uncle Abu Ṭālib ibn 'Abd al-Muṭṭalib.
- Ibn Abi Ḥusayn narrated: 'Durrah bint Abu Lahab was married to al-Ḥārith ibn 'Abdullāh ibn Nawfal, and she gave him his three sons: 'Uqbah, al-Walīd and Abu Muslim. She then migrated to Madinah, and people taunted her about her father. She went to God's Messenger and said: "Messenger of God, am I the only one born to unbelievers?" He said: "What has happened?" She said: "The people of Madinah hurt me about my parents." The Prophet said to her: "When you come to the Ẓuhr Prayer, take a position where I can see you." The Prophet (peace be upon him) led the Ẓuhr Prayer then turned towards the people and said: "People, do you all have ancestors and I have none?" 'Umar ibn al-Khaṭṭāb rose quickly and said to him: "May God displease anyone who caused your displeasure." The Prophet said: "This one is the daughter of my uncle. Let no one say to her anything other than good."' (Related by al-Ṭabrānī) Durrah was the Prophet's cousin, as her father was Abu Lahab ibn 'Abd al-Muṭṭalib.
- Umm al-Faḍl narrated: 'A bedouin entered to meet God's Messenger (peace be upon him) as he was in my home. He said: "Messenger of God, I have been married and then married another woman. My first wife claimed that she breastfed my new wife one or two feeds." The Prophet said: "One or two feeds do not block marriage."' (Related by Muslim) Umm al-Faḍl was the wife of the Prophet's uncle, al-'Abbās ibn 'Abd al-Muṭṭalib.
- Jābir ibn 'Abdullāh narrated that the Prophet said to Asmā' bint 'Umays: "Why are my brother's children so thin? [He

meant Ja'far ibn Abu Ṭālib's children.] Are they in poverty?" She said: "No, but the evil eye may affect them." He said: "Supplicate for them." She read out [her supplication] to him and he said: "Supplicate for them."' (Related by Muslim) Asmā' bint 'Umays was Ja'far's wife and Ja'far's father was Abu Ṭālib, the Prophet's uncle.

- 'Ā'ishah narrated: 'Hālah bint Khuwaylid, Khadījah's sister, sought permission to enter the Prophet's home. He recognized Khadījah's way of seeking permission and he was agitated. He said: "My Lord, let it be Hālah."'

3. Encouraging women's participation in social life
Such participation will inevitably lead to meetings between men and women in good and beneficial areas. By contrast, covering women's faces encourages women to remain in isolation and this leads her to stay away from participation in any activity that requires mixing with men, regardless of the interests that are served by such participation. Such interests include facilitating matters of daily life, enabling women to develop and improve their characters as they can attend scholars' circles and study groups, as well as other good activities run by men. Women will also be able to contribute to professional, social or political activities that benefit society. The best evidence to prove our view is the fact that women participated in such activities during the Prophet's lifetime, as we have illustrated in Volumes 2 and 3 of this series citing numerous actual cases. Had women been covering their faces, they would not have dared to meet men in all areas of public and private life and participate with them in many aspects of professional, social and political activity.
4. Uncovering women's faces enhances society's role as watch guard
One of the features of Islamic society is that it exercises its role as watch guard and upholds the principle of denouncing and prohibiting what is evil. Every individual in Muslim society is fully aware of this and keen to protect their individual and family

reputation. Thus, it helps to protect individuals from falling into tempting, sinful action. In this way, society strengthens the role of personal conscience and helps individuals to steer away from unacceptable behaviour. A woman who goes about with her face uncovered is keen not to be seen by anyone, least of all her relatives, in an unbecoming situation. She does not even wish to be seen by a stranger in such a situation, because he may subsequently identify her. Thus, she watches her behaviour in order to maintain her respectable social standing. If she goes about with her face covered, she has no fear of being identified, and thus the temptation to be adventurous is much stronger.

5. Helping social security

   When a woman covers her face she actually hides herself completely, particularly in our modern urban societies which are overcrowded with a large mixture of people who do not know one another. Yet in these societies women frequently go out, either to work or to attend to their family needs. In such a society, hiding women may cause different harmful effects and present dangers to social security. For example, some evil people may wear women's clothes and infiltrate women's gathering places. People who are close to the scene of a crime may not be able to identify the criminals when they act as witnesses.

   However, a veil that leaves the woman's eyes and the area around them visible is often worn in some small and confined societies, such as those of Bedouin tribes. Such a veil may not have any negative effect on the aspects of a social watch guard and security, because everyone knows most people. They belong to the same tribe and they have close family relations with most of those around them. Moreover, in such environments, the veil is often looked upon as a type of clothing that gives a touch of beauty. It does not withhold women from participating in all areas of social life without hesitation or embarrassment.

6. Normal face uncovering helps to reduce temptation
It is well known that familiarity with something reduces its effect and attraction. When a Muslim man sees women going about with their faces uncovered, their appeal is naturally reduced. There is no doubt that the man will continue to need to control himself, but what we are talking about is a reduction, not disappearance, of appeal and temptation. By contrast, a Muslim who is accustomed to seeing women covering their faces will find the temptation much stronger if he happens to see a woman with her face exposed. In such connection Ibn Bādīs said: 'Among Muslims today are groups – mostly not town or village dwellers [i.e. Bedouin people] – who are used to seeing women going about with their faces uncovered. They pay little attention to them. Such women are not to be required to cover their faces. However, Muslims continue to be required to lower their gaze and not to stare at women. Among Muslims, also groups – mostly town and village dwellers – who are used to seeing women covering their faces, when a woman goes out with her face uncovered, she is stared at.'

I say to those who are used to seeing women covering their faces in some Muslim societies that in order to achieve the advantages of uncovering women's faces that this process should be gradual. We need to give men the time to become used to seeing women going out with their faces uncovered.

7. Face uncovering helps women to maintain modesty
When a woman covers her face fully, including her eyes, she may become more forward in looking at men. She may be encouraged, particularly if she is weak in character, to stare hard, realizing that no one is seeing her. Only a woman who has attained a high degree of piety and purity is free of such temptation. By contrast, a woman with an uncovered face is too shy to do this in public.

8. Face uncovering promotes mental health
   When women do not cover their faces, people in society remain attracted to the other sex. This means that the natural desire which God has given all people continues to run its natural course and does not deviate into attraction towards the same sex. People with strong character continue to steer away from error, putting effort into this, but such people are the minority in society. The majority have weaker character. When women uncover their faces, the weaker elements may commit some minor sins, and they may even commit the major sin, but this will mostly be infrequent. However, they will always maintain the natural way.

   On the other hand, when women cover their faces and all avenues to see the other sex are closed, many people will turn towards the same sex, where there are no checks and controls. This phenomenon is well known in our present time and throughout history. I witnessed both situations when I lived in two different types of society. When I was in a society where women went about with their faces exposed and they participated in a different aspect of social life, homosexual tendencies were rare. But when I lived in a society where women were totally isolated from men's society, many young men turned towards the same sex.

   Here we are talking about our own time and what we have seen and known. Yet we have what refers to the same deviant tendency in earlier periods, which they called 'association with beardless boys'. It is useful to quote from Ibn Taymiyyah's fatwas some of his strong warnings about this. It shows that it was in some degree a social phenomenon. This deviant practice even tempted some Sufis:

Shaykh al-Islam Ibn Taymiyyah was asked about the practice of some people who associate with young men. In his answer he said:

> All praise be to God. Association with beardless boys, and with one of them in particular as they actually do, in addition to being alone with a handsome boy staying overnight with him at times are grave, sinful actions in Islam, Judaism, Christianity and other faiths as well. If such association does not involve the forbidden sexual act, it is susceptible to it and may lead to it. Therefore, devout, God-fearing scholars warned against it. Fatḥ al-Mūṣilī said: 'I met thirty of the *abdāl*[6], and every single one of them warned me, on leaving him, against association with young lads.' Maʿrūf al-Karkhī said that they used to prohibit it. A distinguished *tābiʿīn* scholar said: 'I do not fear for a devout young man that a wild beast sits with him as much as I fear that a young boy sits with him.' Sufyān al-Thawrī and Bishr al-Ḥāfī said: 'One whispering devil comes with a woman, but with a young boy come two devils.'

Shaykh al-Islam was also asked about some people who associate with beardless young boys, and that they may kiss the boy or be in bed with him. They claim that they associate with the boy for God's sake and they do not consider this to be sinful or shameful. They say that they associate with them for no ill purpose. The boy's father, uncle and brother may know of this and they do not object. What is the divine ruling on such people? How should a Muslim treat them? He answered:

> All praise be to God. A beardless handsome lad should be treated like an unrelated woman in many respects. It is prohibited to kiss him with enjoyment. Indeed, no one should kiss him except those who are his immediate relatives, such as his father and siblings. It is forbidden to look at him feeling sexual desire. Indeed the majority of

6. This is a title Sufis give to some of their most senior people. – Author's note.

> scholars say that it is forbidden to look at him if one fears that such a feeling may be associated with his look. He may be looked at when needed, such as doing some business, for giving a testimony for or against him and the like.
>
> A hadith related in the *Sunan* quotes the Prophet: 'If you find a person doing as Lot's people used to do, kill both parties.' Therefore, the Prophet's companions agreed that both are punishable by death, but they differed in the way this should be done. Some said by stoning, while others said that such a person should be thrown from the top of the highest wall in town and stones should be hurled on him as he is falling. Others still said that the punishment is death by burning. The majority of early and later scholars make stoning the punishment, whether the offenders were married or not, free men or slaves, and even if one of them is a slave of the other.

I may add that if the early scholars were of the view that both parties are to be punished by stoning, whether they are married or unmarried, this shows that committing a sin with a woman, even amounting to fornication, is a lesser offence than doing it with a boy. The punishment of a fornicating man and woman who are unmarried is one hundred lashes. It is definitely not stoning.

Secondary evidence 5: Covering the woman's face causes hardship and uncovering it makes things easier

God says: 'He has laid no hardship on you in anything that pertains to religion.' (22: 78). One of the Fiqh rules mentioned by scholars says: 'Hardship calls for relaxation'. Ibn Qudāmah says in *al-Mughnī*: 'Some of our [Ḥanbalī] scholars said that the entire body of a woman is *'awrah*, because a hadith is narrated quoting the Prophet as saying: "A woman is *'awrah*," but a concession is granted allowing women to uncover their faces and hands because covering them involves real hardship.' Ibn Taymiyyah said: 'To cover these [meaning a woman's face and hands] during prayer causes real and great hardship.' Needless to say, the hardship is much greater if they are to be covered in all other situations. Here are some aspects of the hardship caused by covering one's face and hands.

- Covering the woman's face reduces the function of senses positioned in the human face. This is bound to cause her hardship. Uncovering her face allows these senses to operate fully, as God granted them. These senses are sight, smell and tasting food and drink. Furthermore, uncovering the face allows breathing and speaking to progress smoothly. Al-Qurṭubī is right as he says: 'There are many benefits and ways of learning in a woman's face.'
- Uncovering the face reduces the severity of climate in tropical areas. To cover her face in such a climate, particularly during the summer, is really hard for a woman. Most Muslim countries have hot climates.

CHAPTER V

Early Scholars' Agreement on Uncovering Women's Faces

Scholars' statements on leaving women's faces uncovered

One: From books of Fiqh

The Ḥanafī School of Fiqh

In *al-Mabsūṭ*, al-Sarakhsī (died 490 AH, 1097 CE) says: 'A woman's head is part of her *'awrah*. God's Messenger (peace be upon him) said: "God does not accept the prayer of a woman who has attained puberty unless she wears a head covering."' He also says: 'It is unanimously agreed that a woman in consecration does not cover her face, although she is a covered *'awrah* and uncovering her face may be a cause of temptation... She is commanded to offer her worship covered in the best way, as we have explained concerning prayer. Therefore, she wears ordinary, sewn garments and shoes, covers her head but does not cover her face.'

'Alī al-Marghīnānī (died 593 AH, 1197 CE) says in *al-Hidāyah*: 'The entire body of a free woman is *'awrah*, apart from her face and hands. This is based on the Prophet's hadith: "The woman is a covered *'awrah*." Those two parts are excepted so as their exposure serves as a test.' In the same book he says: 'A woman in consecration does not cover her face, although uncovering it may be a cause of temptation.'

Muhammad al-Bābartī (died 786 AH, 1384 CE) writes in his book *Sharḥ al-'Ināyah 'ala al-Hidāyah*: 'The statement "Those two parts are excepted so as their exposure serves as a test" refers to the fact that a woman finds it necessary to do things with her own hands. She also feels the need to uncover her face, particularly in court and when she testifies...' Al-Ḥasan reports from Abu Ḥanīfah that 'the feet are not part of the *'awrah*... A woman cannot avoid exposing her feet when she walks, whether bare-foot or wearing sandals.'

In *Fatḥ al-Qadīr* by al-Kamāl ibn al-Hammām (died 681 AH 1283 CE) writes: 'The difference between man and woman is marked by covering the head. The man's consecration is centred in his head, and he reveals it, while the woman's consecration is in her face and she reveals it.'

The Mālikī School

In *al-Muwaṭṭa'* by Imam Mālik (died 179 AH, 795 CE): Mālik was asked whether a woman may eat with a man who is not her unmarriageable relative or with her slave? He said: 'There is no harm in this, if it is in a way that is normally accepted for women to eat with such men [meaning a way that is generally acceptable to them].' He added: 'A woman may eat with her husband and whoever is eating with him.'

Abu al-Walīd al-Bājī (died 494 AH, 1101 CE), the author of *al-Muntaqā*, an explanation of *al-Muwaṭṭa'* said: 'His words, "a woman may eat with her husband and whoever is eating with him," necessarily means that it is permissible for a man to look at a woman's face and hands, because these will appear when he is eating with her. Scholars have differed on this point, but the reference here is to God's order that women must 'not reveal their adornments except what may ordinarily appear thereof.' (24: 31) 'Abdullāh ibn Mas'ūd said: 'Adornment is of two types: apparent, which is clothing...' However, Sa'īd ibn Jubayr quotes Ibn 'Abbās: 'What may ordinarily appear thereof' means her face and hands. The same is expressed by 'Aṭā'. Ibn Bukayr mentions that it is Māik's view.'

Abu al-Qāsim al-'Abdarī, the author of *al-Tāj wal-Iklīl* said in his comments on what Mālik said: 'This means that a woman may expose her face and hands before a man who is a stranger. Eating is not conceivable without revealing them.'

Also in *al-Muwaṭṭa'*: 'Mālik said that he heard scholars say: "If a woman dies and there are no women to give her her final bath, and there is neither an immediate *maḥram* relative whom she could not marry nor her husband to give her that bath, a dry ablution, i.e. *tayammum*, is performed for her, wiping her face and hands with light dust."'

In *Bidāyat al-Mujtahid,* Ibn Rushd (died 595 AH, 1198 CE) says about Mālik's view: 'Looking at the places of dry ablution by both men and women is permissible. Therefore, Mālik felt it necessary that a woman who dies with only men around should be given a dry ablution to her face and hands only, as these are not part of her *'awrah*.'

In *al-Mudawwanah al-Kubrā*: 'Mālik said that if a woman prays with her hair, chest, feet or wrists kept visible, she should repeat her prayer as long as its time has not lapsed.' The fact that Imam Mālik left out the woman's face in the list of the parts of a woman's body requiring repeating the prayer, if they are left apparent, indicates that it is permissible to reveal her face during prayer and that it is not part of her *'awrah*.

In *al-Muntaqā Sharḥ al-Muwaṭṭa'*: 'For a free woman, all her body is *'awrah* except her face and hands... Our scholars cite in evidence God's order that women must "not reveal their adornments except what may ordinarily appear thereof" (24: 31). They said that what ordinarily appears is her face and two hands. The majority of Qur'anic commentators give the same meaning. Another indication is that these parts must be uncovered during consecration, which means that they are not *'awrah*, in the same way as a man's face is not part of his *'awrah*.'

In *al-Kāfi*, by Ibn 'Abd al-Barr (died 463 AH 1071 CE) says: 'The minimum required of a free woman in her prayer is what covers all her body except her face and hands. Her consecration for hajj or 'umrah is the same way. The rest of her body is *'awrah*.'

In *al-Tamhīd* also by Ibn 'Abd al-Barr: 'All the woman's body except her face and hands is *'awrah*, confirmed by the fact that she may not reveal her body during prayer.' He also says: 'A free woman is all *'awrah*, except her face and hands. This is unanimously agreed upon.' Also, 'That 'Ā'ishah combed the Prophet's hair when he was in *i'tikāf* proves that a woman's hands are not part of her *'awrah*. Had they been *'awrah*, she would not have touched his body with her hands whilst he was in *i'tikāf*. This is further evidenced by the fact that a woman is not allowed to wear gloves when she is in consecration. She is commanded to cover all her body except her face and hands. She is also commanded to reveal these during her prayer. All this proves that these parts are not *'awrah*. This is to us the most correct of all that is said in this connection'.

We may add that Imam Mālik's view regarding a woman's *'awrah* is particularly important because he does not just rely on the authentic hadiths but also on the practice of the people of Madinah. On the importance of the practice of the people of Madinah, Justice Ibn Rushd says:

To my mind, treating the practice of the people of Madinah as religious evidence is akin to the common practice, or *'umūm al-balwā*, which is upheld by Abu Ḥanīfah. It means that such practices which are often repeated and its causes often occurring could not have been abrogated and continue to be practised by the people of Madinah who have been keen to implement the Sunnah, generation after generation. This is indeed stronger evidence than the principle of common practice upheld by Abu Ḥanīfah. The people of Madinah are more likely to be aware of such matters than other communities whose practice Abu Ḥanīfah upholds as a means of transmission. In short, action is certainly a supporting evidence if it is related to what is transmitted: if the two [i.e. the supporting evidence and the transmitted statement] are in agreement, this makes for a strong probability and if they are in disagreement, it makes for weak probability. As for whether this supporting evidence can be sufficient to reject singly-reported authentic hadiths is a debatable matter. It may attain that in some matters but not in others, because matters of common practice differ in how far they spread. The point here is that in the case of a widely needed and frequently occurring action, its single-reporting indicates lack of authenticity, because it does not become widely known verbally or practically. It suggests one of two things: either it has been abrogated or there is some flaw in its reporting.

Ibn Taymiyyah said: 'If two pieces of evidence, such as two hadiths or two analogies, pertain to the same question and they are mutually contradictory, and it is unknown which of them is weightier, but one is adopted by the people of Madinah, then this constitutes a case of controversy. Mālik and al-Shāfi'ī consider that the practice of the people of Madinah provides added weight. Abu Ḥanīfah takes the opposite view. Ḥanbalī scholars hold two different views: the first is that it does not add weight, which is the view of Justice Abu Ya'lā and Ibn 'Aqīl, and the second is stated by Abu al-Khaṭṭāb and others saying that it adds weight. It is said that this is the view quoted from Ahmad, as he says: 'If the people of Madinah act on the basis of a hadith, this is the ultimate to be sought. He used to give rulings on the lines of the Madinah people's practice.'

The Shāfi'ī School

In *al-Umm*, Imam al-Shāfi'ī (died 204 AH, 820 CE) wrote: 'Both man and woman must cover their *'awrah* when they pray... Whatever covers the *'awrah* and is not impure, i.e. *najis*, is suitable for prayer. A man's *'awrah* is from his waist line, just below the navel down to his knees... A woman covers all her body when she prays except her face and hands... It is sufficient for man and woman that each of them covers the *'awrah* when they pray. The man's *'awrah* is what I mentioned and the woman's *'awrah* is all her body except her face and hands.'

Al-Shīrāzī (died 476 AH, 1084 CE) wrote in *al-Muhadhdhab*: 'A free woman's *'awrah* is all her body except her face and hands. This is based on God's order that women must "not reveal their adornments except what may ordinarily appear thereof" (24: 31). Ibn 'Abbās explains that this refers to her face and hands. Moreover, the Prophet (peace be upon him) ordered women in consecration not to weir a veil or gloves. Had the woman's face and hands been *'awrah*, covering them [during consecration] would not have been forbidden. Further, there is need to uncover the woman's face when she buys or sells, and to uncover her hands when she gives or takes. Therefore, these parts of the body are not included in the *'awrah*. In another place in this book, the author writes: 'If a man wants to marry a woman, he may look at her face and hands. He should not look at other parts because they are *'awrah*.'

In *al-Majmū'*, Imam al-Nawawī (died 676 AH, 1278 CE) wrote: 'A woman's *'awrah* is all her body except her face and hands.'

The Ḥanbalī School

In *al-Mukhtaṣar* by al-Khiraqī (died 344 AH, 956 CE) we read: 'If during prayer any part of the woman's body other than her face is exposed, she must repeat her prayer.'

In *al-Hidāyah*, al-Kalwadhānī (died 510 AH, 1117 CE) wrote: 'The woman's *'awrah* is all her body except her face, but two views are expressed regarding her hands.'

Ibn Hubayrah (died 560 AH, 1165 CE) wrote in *al-Ifṣāḥ 'an Ma'ānī al-Ṣiḥāḥ*: 'The extent of the *'awrah*: ... Ahmad said in one of two views reported from him: "All her body is *'awrah* except her face and hands..." The other reported view makes her face the only exception. This is the better known view, and the one chosen by al-Khiraqī.'

He also writes: 'They agree that if a man wants to marry a woman, he may look at what is not *'awrah* of her body... We explain in the 'Book of Prayer' the differences of the four schools regarding the extent of the *'awrah*.'

In *al-Mughnī* by Ibn Qudāmah (died 620 AH, 1223 CE) we read the following:

- There is no disagreement in our school that a woman may uncover her face during prayer... and that she may not reveal any part of her body other than her face and hands. However, there are two views concerning her hands.
- Clothes are excepted from what is prohibited during consecration, because a woman needs clothes to cover her *'awrah*, which is all her body except her face.
- There is no difference among scholars that it is permissible to look at the face of the woman one intends to marry, because the face is not *'awrah*, while it is the place of her attractions and what catches the eye.

Ibn Qudāmah also cites the hadith that says: 'When a woman has attained puberty, it is not permissible for any part of her body to be seen, except this and this, pointing to his face and hands.' Ibn Qudāmah adds: 'Ahmad cites this hadith as evidence.'

Majd al-Dīn 'Abd al-Salām ibn Taymiyyah (died 652 AH, 1254 CE) wrote in his *al-Muḥarrar fi al-Fiqh*: 'All the body of a free woman is *'awrah* except her face, but there are two views concerning her hands.'

The Ẓāhirī School:

Ibn Ḥazm (died 456 AH 1064 CE) wrote in *al-Muḥallā*: 'God says concerning women: "And tell believing women... not to display their charms except what may ordinarily appear thereof. Let them draw their head-coverings over their bosoms and not display their charms to any but their husbands..." God commands women to draw their head-coverings over their bosoms. This is a clear statement requiring the covering of the *'awrah*, neck and chest. It also includes clear permission to leave the face uncovered. Nothing other than this may be gathered from this text.'

Ibn Ḥazm mentions the hadith narrated by Ibn 'Abbās speaking of the Eid Prayer, which includes: '... I saw them holding them [i.e. their jewellery] in their hands and throwing them in Bilāl's robe.' He then adds: 'We note that Ibn 'Abbās saw their hands in the presence of God's Messenger (peace be upon him). Thus, it is right to say that a woman's hands and face are not *'awrah*. The rest of her body she must cover.'

Ibn Ḥazm further cites the hadith mentioning the woman from Khath'am and comments: 'Had the woman's face been *'awrah*, God's Messenger would not have approved her leaving her face uncovered in the presence of men. He would have ordered her to draw part of her top clothing over her face. Had her face been covered Ibn 'Abbās would not have known whether she was pretty or ugly.'

Two: Scholars explain the views of Fiqh schools

Ibn ʿAbd al-Barr says in *al-Tamhīd*: 'Mālik, Abu Ḥanīfah, al-Shāfiʿī and their disciples, as well as al-Awzāʿī and Abu Thawr said: "A woman is obligated to cover herself except her face and hands..." Scholars are unanimous that a woman must offer her obligatory prayers with her hands and face uncovered, placing them on the floor. They are also unanimous that she may not wear a veil when praying and she need not wear gloves. This is the clearest evidence that these are not part of her *ʿawrah*.'

Al-Baghawī (died 516 AH, 1122 CE) said in *Sharḥ al-Sunnah*: 'A free woman must cover her body in prayer, apart from her face and hands up to her elbows. He reports this from Ibn ʿAbbās, and it is the view of al-Awzāʿī and al-Shāfiʿī'.

Al-Baghawī also said: Chapter: on looking at a woman one intends to marry... 'Some scholars say: If a man intends to marry a woman, he may look at her. This is the view of al-Thawrī, al-Shāfiʿī, Ahmad and Isḥāq. He may do so whether she agrees or not. However, he may only look at her face and hands. It is not permissible for him to look at her with her head uncovered, or to look at any part of her *ʿawrah*. Al-Awzāʿī said: "He may only look at her face."'

In *Bidāyat al-Mujtahid* Ibn Rushd says: 'The extent of a woman's *ʿawrah*: Most scholars agree that all her body is *ʿawrah* except her face and hands. Abu Ḥanīfah says that her feet are also not *ʿawrah*, while Abu Bakr ibn ʿAbd al-Raḥmān and Ahmad consider all her body to be *ʿawrah*.'

Ibn Qudāmah said in *al-Mughnī*: 'Abu Ḥanīfah said: "The two feet of a woman are not *ʿawrah*, because they appear in most cases. Therefore, they are to be treated like her face..." Mālik, al-Awzāʿī and al-Shāfiʿī said that all the woman's body is *ʿawrah* except her face and hands.'

Three: Statements by some scholars

Ibn Baṭṭāl (died 449 AH, 1063 CE) said: 'The hadith concerning the woman from Khath'am gives an order to lower one's gaze so as not to yield to temptation... The hadith provides evidence that female believers are not included in the order given to the Prophet's wives to remain behind a screen. Had it been applicable to all women, the Prophet would have ordered the Khath'amī woman to cover herself and he would not have turned al-Faḍl's face away from her... It also provides evidence that it is not obligatory for a woman to cover her face... and that the order, "Say to believing men to lower their gaze," applies as a duty but does not include the woman's face.'

Al-Mutawallī (died 478 AH, 1086 CE) said: 'If the woman is pretty and one fears temptation, greeting is not appropriate, neither to begin with nor to respond to. If either one offers the greeting, the other is discouraged from replying. If the woman is elderly and there is no chance of temptation, greeting is permissible.' Ibn Ḥajar comments on this view by al-Mutawallī who is a distinguished Shāfi'ī scholar, saying: 'The difference between this view and that of the Mālikī scholars, who differentiate between young and elderly women, are the details given in the case of a younger woman and whether she is pretty or not. Beauty invites temptation, which is not the case in all younger women.' Again I say: how can one distinguish a pretty young woman from a plain one unless their faces are uncovered?

Al-Baghawī said: 'In the case of a woman with a man, if she is a free woman, unrelated to him, all her body is *'awrah* and he may not look at any part of her except her face and two hands, up to the elbows. God says that women must "not reveal their adornments except what may ordinarily appear thereof". In explanation it is said that this exception refers to the woman's face and hands. The man must further lower his gaze so that he would not gaze at her face and hands when he fears temptation. God says: "Tell the believers to lower their gaze and be mindful of their chastity."'

Justice ‘Iyāḍ (died 544 AH, 1150 CE) said: ‘The Prophet’s wives were given a special order to cover their faces and hands... They could not show themselves, even when fully covered, except for what was a necessity, such as going out to relieve themselves.’ He also said: ‘The *ḥijāb* order is another thing that applied to the Prophet’s wives alone. It was their duty, with no difference of views regarding their faces and hands. They could not uncover these for giving testimony or for any other need.’

Ibn Rushd said: ‘Scholars generally say that a woman in mourning should refrain from wearing adornments that may be appealing to men, such as jewellery and kohl, except articles without ornaments, and also from wearing colourful clothes, except black... Generally speaking, scholars’ views on what a woman in mourning should avoid are very close, and they refer in general to what is attractive to men...’ He also said: ‘... Scholars who apply to divorced women the same rules as those applicable to widows in their waiting period rely on the underlying meaning. It seems that ‘mourning’ refers to ensure that men are not attracted to a woman during her waiting period, nor she be attracted to them. This is to prevent causes leading to what is forbidden and to ensure that cases of parenthood are untampered with.’

Needless to say, men may be attracted to a woman in mourning if she has her face and hands uncovered, so as to see what she is wearing of kohl or makeup and what she has on her hands of jewellery and henna.

Ibn Daqīq al-‘Īd (died 702 AH, 1303 CE) said: ‘Some limit the hadith which says: “Do not stop female servants of God from frequenting God’s mosques,” saying that a pretty woman who is well known must not go out to the mosque.’

My question here is: how is her beauty to be known unless her face is uncovered?

Now that we have looked at the views of the four schools of Fiqh, quoting the approved books in each school, and quoting what leading scholars attribute to the founders of such schools, adding the views of some highly distinguished scholars, we conclude by saying that the major books written by highly distinguished scholars in each school assert that the woman's face is not *'awrah*. These books include:

- In the Ḥanafī School: *al-Mabsūṭ*, *al-Hidāyah* and *Fatḥ al-Qadīr*;
- In the Mālikī School: *al-Muwaṭṭa'*, *al-Mudawwanah al-Kubrā*, *al-Muntaqā*, *al-Tamhīd* and *al-Kāfī*;
- In the Shāfi'ī School: *al-Umm*, *al-Muhadhdhab* and *al-Majmū'*;
- In the Ḥanbalī School: *Mukhtaṣar al-Khiraqī*, *al-Hidāyah*, *al-Ifṣāḥ 'an Ma'ānī al-Ṣiḥāḥ*, *al-Mughnī* and *al-Muḥarrar fi al-Fiqh*, and
- In the Ẓāhirī School: *al-Muḥallā*.

Early scholars' agreement on the status of women's faces

The four Imams, the founders of the four schools of Fiqh, and indeed other leading scholars agree that a woman's face is not part of her *'awrah*. We have already established this agreement with quotations from the approved sources of these schools and major works. This general agreement is confirmed by leading scholars of Qur'anic commentary, Hadith and Fiqh. Such agreement is so widespread as to be described by some of these leading scholars as 'unanimity'.

Among leading Qur'anic commentators, Imam al-Ṭabarī (died 310 AH, 923 CE) said: 'The view closest to the truth is that of scholars who say that the reference in the Qur'anic verse to what may be seen of a woman's charms, or adornments, applies to her face and hands... We say that this is closest to the truth because they are all unanimous that everyone must cover their *'awrah* during prayer and that a woman keeps her face and hands uncovered during prayer, but covers the rest of her body... As this is their unanimous view, it becomes clear that she uncovers of her body what is not *'awrah*, in the same way as this is the case with men. What is not *'awrah* is not forbidden to be shown.'

And among leading Hadith scholars, Ibn Baṭṭāl said: 'Covering her face is not obligatory for a woman, as scholars are unanimous that a woman may uncover her face during prayer, even though strangers may see her.'

Among leading Ḥanafī scholars, al-Sarakhsī says: 'It is unanimously agreed that a woman in consecration does not cover her face, although she is a covered *'awrah*... She is commanded to offer her worship covered in the best way, as we have explained concerning prayer.'

Among leading Mālikī scholars, Ibn 'Abd al-Barr says: 'A free woman is all *'awrah*, except her face and hands. This is unanimously agreed upon... She is commanded to offer her worship covered in the best way, as we have explained concerning prayer.'

Justice 'Iyāḍ said: 'There is no disagreement that the obligation to cover their faces applies particularly to the Prophet's wives... Scholars differ as to whether it is recommended in the case of other women.'

Among the leading Shāfi'ī scholars, al-Qaffāl said: 'Since the exposure of a Muslim woman's face and hands is akin to necessity, scholars agree that they are not part of a woman's *'awrah*. As for the feet, uncovering them is not necessary. Hence, scholars differ as to whether they are part of the woman's *'awrah*.'

Al-Nawawī said: 'What is best-known in our school is that the *'awrah* of a free woman is all her body except her face and hands.

All this is agreed upon by Mālik and other scholars, and it is one view attributed to Ahmad... Others who said that a free woman's '*awrah* is all her body except her face and hands include al-Awzāʿī and Abu Thawr. Abu Ḥanīfah, al-Thawrī and al-Muzanī said that her feet are also not '*awrah*. Ahmad said that her '*awrah* covers all her body except only her face.' Thus, al-Nawawī confirms agreement as he mentions the four Imams and adds al-Awzāʿī, Abu Thawr, al-Thawrī and al-Muzanī.

Among the leading Ḥanbalī scholars, Ibn Hubayrah said: 'Abu Ḥanīfah said that all the body of a woman is '*awrah* except her face, hands and feet... Mālik and al-Shāfiʿī said that all her body is '*awrah* except her face and hands. Ahmad said in one of two views reported from him: All her body is '*awrah* except her face and hands, agreeing with them. The other reported view makes her face the only exception. This is the better known view.' Thus, Ibn Hubayrah also confirms that all four Imams agree on the extent of the woman's '*awrah*.

Ibn Qudāmah said: 'There is no disagreement among scholars that it is permissible to look at the face of a woman who is proposed to for marriage, because the face is not part of the woman's '*awrah*'. He also says: 'All scholars agree that a woman may pray with her face uncovered.'

Ibn Qudāmah further says that those who say that all of a woman's body is '*awrah* except her face and hands are Abu Ḥanīfah, Mālik, al-Awzāʿī and al-Shāfiʿī, in addition to Imam Ahmad. It is not possible that such leading scholars would confirm such agreement in a matter that is common to all people on the basis of scholarly reasoning which may be right or wrong. This means that such agreement must be based on sure knowledge that is passed on from one generation to another. This is an aspect of God's grace bestowed on the Muslim community.

It is about such agreement by early distinguished scholars that Ibn al-Qayyim says in his book *I'lām al-Muwaqqi'īn*: 'The third type of praised view is that on which the Muslim community agrees, and which is passed on from early to later generations. What they agree upon can be nothing but correct'.

Ibn Taymiyyah acknowledges agreement, but

Ibn Taymiyyah said: 'As for covering these (meaning the woman's face and hands) during prayer, it is not a duty, as all Muslims agree.'

Since covering is not a duty 'as all Muslims agree', then there is no harm in uncovering these parts. This is close to what early scholars have mentioned as unanimously agreed upon. However, Imam Ibn Taymiyyah limits the permissibility of uncovering them to prayer. We will mention the details of this claim, but we will say briefly here that it is based on saying that what scholars have said about covering in prayer is limited to prayer only and cannot be extended to other times, in front of men. I think we have done enough to refute this claim. We have established on the basis of what leading scholars of Qur'anic commentary, Hadith and Fiqh say that the *'awrah* is the same in all cases. Therefore, what may be uncovered in prayer may remain so at other times. Therefore, we say that Ibn Taymiyyah has acknowledged agreement on the permissibility of uncovering women's faces. However, his claim that this permissibility is limited to prayer only does not hold, and it cannot invalidate the scholars' agreement. What we are saying is based on the detailed evidence we have mentioned.

Does an odd view detract from agreement by early scholars?

We quoted what leading scholars of different Fiqh schools, including the Ḥanbalī School, said about the legitimacy of leaving the woman's face uncovered. We also quoted what distinguished scholars said about the general agreement, or unanimity, of early scholars that a woman's face is not part of her *'awrah*. However, we are not unaware of an odd view stated by some scholars saying that every part of the woman's body, including her nails, are *'awrah*. A number of scholars mention this odd view:

Ibn 'Abd al-Barr said:[7] 'Abu Bakr ibn 'Abd al-Raḥmān ibn al-Ḥārith said: "Every part of the woman's body is *'awrah*, even her nails..." Abu al-Walīd al-Bājī said: "Some people take the view that she must cover all her body." Ibn Rushd said: "Abu Bakr ibn 'Abd al-Raḥmān and Ahmad have taken the view that all the woman's body is *'awrah*." Ibn Qudāmah says: "Some of our scholars said that all the woman's body is *'awrah* because a hadith narrated from the Prophet says: "The woman is *'awrah*." This is the view of Abu Bakr ibn al-Ḥārith ibn Hishām who says that the woman is totally *'awrah*, even her nails. Al-Nawawī said: "Al-Māwardī and al-Mutawallī narrated from Abu Bakr ibn 'Abd al-Raḥmān of the *tābi'īn* that the woman's body is all *'awrah*, including her nails."'

We have the following observations about these statements. First, all of them attribute the view that the whole body of a woman is *'awrah* to Abu Bakr ibn 'Abd al-Raḥmān, with the exception of Abu al-Walīd al-Bājī who did not mention a person, but said, 'some people'.

Secondly, Ibn Rushd adds Imam Ahmad to Abu Bakr ibn 'Abd al-Raḥmān. However, Ibn Qudāmah, who is a distinguished Ḥanbalī scholar, said that the Ḥanbalī School does not differ from others that a woman reveals her face during prayer. Therefore, we think that the fact that Ibn Rushd and others attribute such a statement to Imam Ahmad may be due to some confusion that occurred due to a report attributed to him implying that a woman must cover all her body in front of men. We shall discuss this confusion shortly when

7. Most of what is quoted here of scholars' statements refers to covering the *'awrah* during prayer. However, since the *'awrah* is the same during prayer and at other times and places – as we shall presently show – these statements mean that a woman's face is not *'awrah* at any time. – Author's note.

we discuss an opinion advanced by some Ḥanbalī scholars which is contrary to the agreement of earlier Fiqh scholars.

Thirdly, most scholars we have quoted imply in some way that the view that all the body of a woman is *'awrah* including her nails is odd. Al-Bājī attributes it to 'some people', leaving them unknown which implies that such a view is both odd and weak. Al-Nawawī mentions first those who state that the face and hands are not part of the woman's *'awrah*: 'the four Imams and also al-Awzā'ī, Abu Thawr, al-Thawrī and al-Muzanī'. He then adds: 'Al-Māwardī and al-Mutawallī narrated from Abu Bakr ibn 'Abd al-Raḥmān of the *tābi'īn* that the woman's body is all *'awrah.'* Ibn Qudāmah mentions that the Ḥanbalī School takes the same view that it is permissible for a woman to uncover herself during prayer, and mentions Māik, al-Shāfi'ī, Abu Ḥanīfah and al-Awzā'ī' as stating that the woman's body is *'awrah* except her face and hands. He then adds: 'Some of our scholars said that all the woman's body is *'awrah*... This is the view of Abu Bakr ibn al-Ḥārith.' Ibn 'Abd al-Barr states most clearly that this view is odd, saying: 'This view of Abu Bakr ibn 'Abd al-Raḥmān ibn al-Ḥārith is alien to the views of scholars.'

Fourthly, having mentioned that some of our scholars say that all the woman's body is *'awrah*, he adds: 'Yet they give her the concession to uncover her face and hands because of the hardship caused by covering these.' This means that those who say that all her body is *'awrah* apply the concession to uncover the face and hands in order to remove the hardship. This is very close to what Ḥanafī scholars said: 'The entire body of a free woman is *'awrah*, apart from her face and hands. This is based on the Prophet's hadith: "The woman is a covered *'awrah*." Those two parts are excepted so as their exposure serves as a test.' On this basis, the question of uncovering the woman's face and hands ranges between complete permissibility and being a concession; it does not range between permissibility and prohibition.

We will now state the attitudes of the Ḥanbalī School of Fiqh and its scholars regarding the agreement that a woman's face is not *'awrah*.

Attitude 1: The Ḥanbalī School is in line with the early scholars' agreement

We have already seen what early Ḥanbalī scholars wrote in the period between the beginning of the fourth century up to the middle of the seventh century of the Hijri calendar (tenth to thirteenth century CE). These show that they agreed with the general consensus that the woman's face is not part of her *'awrah*.

Attitude 2: An opposite view suggested by some Ḥanbalī scholars

The gist of the matter is since the middle of the seventh century (thirteenth century CE) a different view took hold.[8] This upholds the apparent meaning of a reported view of Imam Ahmad stating that a Muslim woman must cover all her body, even her nails. This report is considered to be 'the best known' one from Ahmad and the 'apparent view of Ahmad's School'. The other report which says it is permissible for a woman to leave her face and hands uncovered was treated as merely 'a second view reported from Ahmad'. Taqiy al-Dīn Ahmad ibn Taymiyyah[9] (died 728 AH, 1328 CE) said:

> What ordinarily appears of a woman's adornment is her top clothing. This is stated by Ibn Mas'ūd and the best known view of Ahmad... Ibn 'Abbās said that a woman's face and

8. This view goes back further than the seventh century, and it is mentioned by Ibn al-Jawzī in his *Zād al-Masīr*, which is a commentary on the Qur'an, attributing it to Justice Abu Ya'lā. It is mentioned in his comments on Verse 24: 31. - Author's note.
9. Reference is made to this scholar when the name 'Ibn Taymiyyah' is mentioned on its own. However, his grandfather 'Abd al-Salām, nicknamed Majd al-Dīn, was a distinguished scholar of the Ḥanbalī School and his father 'Abd al-Ḥalīm was also a scholar, nicknamed Shihāb al-Dīn. Ibn Taymiyyah, the grandson, is more famous than both his father and grandfather, and he was given the title Shaykh al-Islam.

> hands are part of her "ordinarily apparent" adornment, and this is the other view reported from Ahmad....
>
> The apparent view of Ahmad's School of Fiqh... is that all a woman's body is *'awrah*, including her nails.

We mentioned earlier the possibility of some confusion occurring as a result of such a report, leading some scholars to consider the woman's face as part of her *'awrah* in the same way as the rest of her body. We consider that such a report, if true, suggests the need to cover the woman's face as a means to prevent causes of temptation, not because it is part of the woman's *'awrah*, although the report does not mention this clearly. If we look at the report in this light, this report (requiring covering the face) does not contradict the report upheld by al-Kalwadhānī, Ibn Hubayrah, Ibn Qudāmah and Majd al-Dīn ibn Taymiyyah, which we mentioned earlier, stating that there is only one report from Ahmad concerning the status of the woman's face and stating that it is not *'awrah*. They are absolutely clear in stating that the Ḥanbalī School has only one view regarding the woman's face, but it has two views regarding the woman's hands.

In giving this interpretation we have two considerations. The first is that we are keen that reports are not set against each other and claimed to be contradictory. The second is that we do not like that these four scholars, highly distinguished as they are, to be accused of being unaware of the different views in their own schools on a matter that is specifically relevant to all women and, indeed, to all men. Every man lives with women: his mother, sisters, wife and daughters. Besides, to give a certain interpretation of this report is not something strange. Indeed, al-Mardāwī, a distinguished Ḥanbalī scholar, (died 885 AH, 1480 CE) quotes al-Zarkashī's different interpretation of the same report. Al-Zarkashī said: 'Ahmad generalizes, saying that all the woman's body is *'awrah*. However, this is understood to mean "except her face" or "when she is not in prayer".'

Attitude 3: An error upheld by Ḥanbalī scholars contradicting the agreement by early scholars:

This is a Fiqh error which claims that the *'awrah* during prayer is different from the *'awrah* in public. This error was committed by some Ḥanbalī scholars as a result of upholding a report attributed to Imam Ahmad stating that a Muslim woman must cover all her body, including her nails. They add their interpretation whereby such covering applies in all situations other than during prayer, as mentioned by al-Mardāwī. It seems that these scholars then felt happy with this preference, treating it as if it is the only view of the Ḥanbalī School. Therefore, they tried to find a way to reconcile this view, which they considered as the only true one, with the statements of early distinguished scholars of their own Ḥanbalī School concerning the condition of covering the *'awrah* during prayer. These scholars said that for a Muslim woman to uncover her face is permissible. Thus, the reconciliation they arrived at suggests that what the early scholars were speaking about was the *'awrah* during prayer only, when it is permissible to uncover the face. Thus, they made a false assumption, suggesting that the *'awrah* is of two types: one that applies during prayer only and the other when one appears in public. They made this applicable to both man and woman. When we look at the books of the Ḥanbalī School dating later than Ibn Hubayrah's *al-Ifṣāḥ*, Ibn Qudāmah's *al-Mughnī* and Majd al-Dīn ibn Taymiyyah's *al-Muḥarrar*, we find that later Ḥanbalī scholars make sure to state that a woman's face is not part of the *'awrah* during prayer, but it is *'awrah* in other situations. We often find them writing about '*'awrah* in prayer' and '*'awrah* in public'.

Thus, for several centuries Ḥanbalī scholars appeared to be in agreement that the *'awrah* in prayer is different from the *'awrah* in public, and that an adult woman's *'awrah* during prayer is all her body except her face. Yet how can they reconcile their agreement with a different report attributed to Imam Ahmad which clearly states that a Muslim woman must cover all her body including her nails during prayer. This report is mentioned by Abu Dāwūd al-Sijistānī, (died 275 AH, 889 CE) the author of the *Sunan* hadith anthology, in his book *Imām Ahmad's Answers*. It says: 'Abu Bakr reported: Abu Dāwūd said: I asked Ahmad: "What may be seen of a woman when she prays?" He said: "Nothing may be seen of her, not even her nails. She must cover everything."'

I suppose it behoves all believers, whether they follow the Ḥanbalī School or other schools, to refer to God's Book and the Prophet's Sunnah in order to determine what God has legislated in all matters. They must not consider the views and rulings of leading scholars as a religion which they follow without thinking. They should treat these in the way Imam al-Shāfi'ī says: as a means to help them understand the Qur'an and the Sunnah. I also feel that it behoves Ḥanbalīs in particular to reflect on what Imam Ahmad (may God be pleased with him) said: 'They used to memorize and write down the Sunnah... As for these questions which are recorded and written down in notebooks: these are unknown to me. Each is simply a view held by someone who may discard it tomorrow. Yet it is quoted and passed on to other people.'

Attitude 4: A wild accusation by Ḥanbalī scholars to continue to reject early scholars' agreed view

This is summed up as a charge by some Ḥanbalī scholars accusing some of the early scholars of confusion between the *'awrah* during prayer and the *'awrah* in public. They made this accusation so that the early scholars are not quoted in support of the view permitting uncovering women's faces. Those who subscribe to this view argue that many early scholars say that a woman may leave her face uncovered when she prays. Had the woman's face been part of her *'awrah*, they would not have permitted its exposure during an act of worship, because worship is performed in the finest of forms, covering all that should be covered. This is the reason for making this accusation: to refute the argument of their opponents who say that a woman may leave her face uncovered.

As far as we know, the accusation was made by two highly distinguished Ḥanbalī scholars who are highly respected by the Muslim community generally. Yet we say: all glory belongs to God. He alone is free of error. We seek God's help as we hope to explain the flaw, or what we think is a flaw, in this accusation.

Imam Ibn Taymiyyah said: 'A number of Fiqh scholars thought that what should be covered during prayer is the same as what should be covered in public, i.e. the *'awrah*... Yet, the *'awrah* in prayer is unrelated to the *'awrah* in public, either directly or indirectly.' And Imam Ibn al-Qayyim said: 'Some Fiqh scholars heard their statement that the whole body of a free woman is *'awrah* except her face and hands... Yet this is applicable to prayer, not in public. The *'awrah* is of two types: one during prayer and another in public.'

This accusation is based on two mistakes. The first is the claim that the *'awrah* is of two types: one during prayer and one in public. This claim is contrary to a basic linguistic rule and a general Fiqh practice. The linguistic rule makes clear that when the word *'awrah* is used, preceded by the definite article 'al', it refers to what is well-known and it signifies what is unbecoming to expose before other people. Thus, linguistically speaking, the general and unqualified usage of the word refers to the *'awrah* in public. The Fiqh practice is that used by Fiqh scholars as they devote a chapter to the conditions for the validity of prayer. In this chapter they include items such as: the time due, facing the *qiblah*, purification of place and clothing, covering the *'awrah*, etc. Thus, *'awrah* is preceded by the definite article 'al' to indicate that it is well-known to all, namely, the *'awrah* in public. Thus, we see that there is only one *'awrah*, defined in clear texts and well-known to people generally. For a man, it is the area between the waist line and the knees, and for a woman, all her body except her face and hands. Fiqh scholars then proceed to explain that covering the *'awrah* is an essential condition for the validity of prayer.

The other mistake is accusing the early scholars of confusing the *'awrah* during prayer with the *'awrah* in public. The fact is that the early scholars did not err and were not confused. They were well aware and absolutely certain that there is only one *'awrah*, which is the one in public. That is the *'awrah* that must be covered from other people's eyes, except in cases of necessity. One is also recommended to cover the *'awrah* from the eyes of angels and jinn. Yet most importantly, a person covers it when alone, in an act of modesty in front of God. The Prophet said the truth when he said to Mu'āwiyah ibn Ḥaydah: 'Cover your *'awrah*, except from your wife or the one your hand possesses.' Mu'āwiyah said: 'Prophet, what if one is alone?' The Prophet said: 'God has more claim to our modesty than people.' (Related by al-Tirmidhī)

It was this *'awrah* that appeared to Adam and Eve when they disobeyed God and ate of the forbidden tree. God said: 'When they both had tasted the fruit of the tree, their nakedness became apparent to them, and they began to cover themselves with leaves from the Garden.' (7: 22) This is the *'awrah* that should be covered and for which God has given us garments to cover: 'Children of Adam, We have sent down to you clothing to cover your nakedness, and garments pleasing to the eye.' (7: 26) It is the one God has commanded us to cover as He said: 'Children of Adam, dress well when you attend any place of worship.' (7: 31)

We should remember here that a man's *'awrah* is the same in all situations, but the woman's *'awrah* is of two levels: one is in her appearance before all men and it is the same as the *'awrah* during prayer, and the other is in her appearance before her immediate relatives whom she may not marry, i.e. *maḥrams*.

Before we proceed further with our evidence that the claim that there are two types of *'awrah* is wrong, we will repeat the statements of some scholars who maintain that what is covered during prayer is the same as what must be covered in public, i.e. the *'awrah*. We apologize for the repetition, but we feel that it is easier for the reader to re-state it here than to refer the reader to former pages. This has been our approach throughout these several volumes.

Those scholars who thought – as Ibn Taymiyyah and Ibn al-Qayyim suggested – that the *'awrah* during prayer is different from that in public are leading scholars of Qur'anic commentary, Hadith or Fiqh. Among the leading Qur'anic commentators are al-Ṭabarī, al-Jaṣṣāṣ, al-Baghawī, Abu Bakr ibn al-'Arabī, al-Qurṭubī and al-Khāzin.

Ibn Jarīr al-Ṭabarī (died 310 AH, 923 CE) said: 'The view closest to the truth is that of scholars who say that the reference in the Qur'anic verse to what may be seen of a woman's charms, or adornments, applies to her face and hands... We say that this is closest to the truth because they are all unanimous that everyone must cover their *'awrah* during prayer and that a woman keeps her face and hands uncovered during prayer, but covers the rest of her body.'

Al-Jaṣṣāṣ (died 370 AH, 981 CE) said: 'It is confirmed that the woman's face and hands are not part of the *'awrah*, which must be covered. A woman prays with her face and hands uncovered. Had they been part of her *'awrah*, she would have had to cover them as she covers all her *'awrah*.'

Al-Baghawī (died 516 AH, 1122 CE) said: 'The concession to leave this uncovered is due to the fact that it is not part of the woman's *'awrah*, and that she is commanded to leave it uncovered when she prays.'

Abu Bakr ibn al-'Arabī (died 543 AH, 1149 CE) said: 'The correct view is that it refers to what is worn on a woman's face and hands, because these two are left uncovered during prayer and consecration as part of these acts of worship.'

Al-Qurṭubī (died 671 AH, 1273 CE) said: 'As it is mostly the case with regard to a woman's face and hands that they are uncovered, habitually and in worship, as in prayer and hajj, the exception in the Qur'anic verse may be rightly taken as referring to them.' (He means by the exception: 'except what may ordinarily appear thereof'.)

Al-Khāzin (died 725 AH, 1326 CE) said: 'The concession to leave this uncovered is due to the fact that it is not part of the woman's *'awrah*, and that she is commanded to leave it uncovered when she prays.'

A leading scholar of Hadith and its meanings, Ibn Baṭṭāl (died 449 AH, 1063 CE) said: 'The hadith concerning the woman from Khath'am provides evidence that it is not obligatory for a woman to cover her face. This is also clear in that scholars are unanimous that a woman may uncover her face during prayer, even though she is seen by strangers.'

A distinguished scholar of the Ḥanafī School, al-Sarakhsī (died 490 AH, 1097 CE) says: 'It is unanimously agreed that a woman in consecration does not cover her face, although she is a covered *'awrah*... She is commanded to offer her worship covered in the best way, as we have explained concerning prayer.'

A distinguished scholar of the Mālikī School, Ibn 'Abd al-Barr (died 463 AH, 1071 CE) said: 'All the woman's body except her face and hands is *'awrah*, confirmed by the fact that she may not reveal her body during prayer.' He also says: 'She is commanded to cover all her body except her face and hands. She is also commanded to reveal these during her prayer. All this proves that these parts are not *'awrah*.'

However, the argument is not based on the high status of these distinguished scholars. Ibn Taymiyyah and Ibn al-Qayyim have the same status, if not higher. The real argument is based on the strength of the evidence we provide and their agreement confirms its strength.

Having perused these comments by such distinguished early scholars of all schools of Fiqh, readers will realize that there is ample evidence confirming that there is only one type of *'awrah*. We have provided the dates that indicate the times of life of these scholars. The fact is that whenever early scholars spoke of the need to cover the *'awrah* during prayer, which is one of the conditions or obligations for its validity, their discussion focused on the *'awrah* in public. Their evidence confirming the *'awrah* during prayer was always the same as the evidence in the Qur'an and the Sunnah describing the *'awrah* in public.

Scholars of later generations agree on the permissibility of uncovering women's faces

It has been the tradition in many areas of the Muslim world that rural women uncover their faces, because they frequently go to the field, the market and on errands. The same applies to the Bedouin women in some countries, such as Algeria. Likewise, the tradition in these countries is that urban women cover their faces, because they remain at home most of the time and rarely go out. Such traditions continued for centuries, particularly in later times, without opposition by scholars. This indicates their approval of uncovering women's faces. It is indeed akin to unanimity by remaining silent.

How is it then that tradition on such a sensitive point as covering or uncovering women's faces differs in urban and rural areas? We say that this is normal, because tradition differs concerning what people are used to doing. In this regard, difference is an aspect of God's grace who has made our religion easy to follow. Besides, it reflects the wisdom of scholars who understand the need for difference. Despite their leaning towards strictness in these later generations and despite their general desire to have faces covered thinking that this prevents causes for temptation, they allowed rural women not to cover their faces, taking into consideration their needs and circumstances. At the same time, they leaned harder on urban women, requiring them to cover their faces when they went out. This strictness did not cause much hardship to urban women because there were plenty of maids and servants that spared the urban woman the need to attend to her family requirements, leaving her to enjoy a life of comfort. Therefore, urban women went out only infrequently, to pay a social visit, attend a celebration or offer condolences, etc. Thus, her outings were short and far between.

It was a recognized tradition in many Muslim areas to distinguish between urban women on the one hand and rural and Bedouin women on the other. Ibn Bādīs said: 'Among Muslims today are groups – mostly not town or village dwellers [i.e. Bedouin people] – who are used to seeing women go about with their faces uncovered. They pay little attention to them. Such women are not to be required to cover their faces. However, Muslims continue to be required to lower their gaze and not to stare at these women. Among Muslims there are also groups – mostly town and village dwellers – who are used to seeing women covering their faces. Therefore, when a woman goes out with her face uncovered, she is stared at and her appearance tempts those who lack fear of God to harass her. This leads to unhealthy gossip about her and her family and clan. Therefore, such women should cover their faces in order to avoid trouble and foul talk.'

Justice 'Iyāḍ confirmed much earlier that 'face-covering, which has been common among urban women in recent times, was no more than a custom approved by scholars as a way of preventing causes of temptation.' He adds that in the hadith mentioning a man's unintentional look at a woman 'we have evidence that a woman is not duty-bound to cover her face when she goes out, but it is desirable for her to do so. Men have the duty of lowering their gaze in all situations, except when there is a legitimate need.' In his commentary on Muslim's *Ṣaḥīḥ* anthology, Imam al-Nawawī quotes this view of Justice 'Iyāḍ and expresses his agreement with it.

Therefore, we need to differentiate between the agreement of early scholars that the woman's face is not *'awrah* and that some scholars prefer face-covering. Some may, on the basis of personal reasoning, consider face-covering a duty to prevent temptation, while others do the same concluding that it is desirable, not a duty, and they express the same basis of preventing temptation. Others still may consider it a permissible tradition and say that what is permissible is good. All these are personal views arrived at through scholarly reasoning, which means that they can be right or wrong. The basis is the evidence they use in support. Moreover, these views may have been arrived at in the light of some temporary considerations. Such discretionary views often differ from time to time.

However, it seems that as time passed and as some scholars took a strict view in favour of face-covering, the claim that the woman's face is *'awrah* was floated, so that such strict scholars could put an end to any ruling that differed with their view, saying that uncovering women's faces is permissible.

As we said earlier, the fact that rural women went out with their faces uncovered and that this has continued in many Muslim countries, for many centuries and until the present day, without opposition by scholars, and indeed by clear approval by many, means that they consider face uncovering legitimate, amounting to agreement by silent unanimity.

To sum up

No verse in the Qur'an clearly states whether women should cover their faces or leave them uncovered. The Prophet's companions and their successors differed in their understanding of the relevant Qur'anic verses (see: Chapter 2). Ibn al-Qayyim says about emulating the Prophet's companions: 'A person may say that he is emulating some of the Prophet's companions, such as one who wishes to follow Ibn Mas'ūd's view that the apparent adornments of a woman are her clothing.' To such a person we say: On what basis have you not taken the views of other companions of the Prophet? Perhaps the view of the one you disregarded is better and more reliable than the view you have adopted. Moreover, no view is considered valid merely on the basis of the status of the one who expresses it, but its validity is determined by the basis on which it relies.

The texts of hadiths which imply the permissibility of the uncovering of the Muslim woman's face are numerous, but those who take the opposite view consider them to imply probability. In our view, they have no justification in making such a claim in respect of many of these texts (see: Chapter 3). A particular hadith is narrated by 'Ā'ishah: 'When a woman has attained puberty, it is not permissible that any part of her body be seen, except this and this, pointing to his face and hands.' This is a *mursal* hadith, but some scholars say that it is strengthened by the expressed views of a number of the Prophet's companions. Al-Bayhaqī says: 'In addition to this *mursal* hadith we have the statements of the Prophet's companions explaining what God has permitted to be seen of apparent charms and adornments. Thus, the statement becomes more solid.' Shaykh Nāṣir al-Albānī comments: 'In his *Tahdhīb Sunan al-Bayhaqī*, al-Dhahabī expresses the same opinion. The Prophet's companions to whom he refers are 'Ā'ishah, Ibn 'Abbās and Ibn 'Umar. They say that the apparent adornment or charms are the woman's face and the hands.' Shaykh al-Albānī also considers this hadith to acquire more strength by the fact that it is reported in several chains of transmission.

Early scholars say that the woman's face is not *'awrah*, although an odd view is expressed by one of the *tābi'īn* who suggests that 'All the woman's body is *'awrah* including her nails.' However, those who uphold this view give women the concession to uncover their faces and hands because covering them involves hardship. The same view is expressed in one report attributed to Imam Ahmad.

The Ḥanbalī School of Fiqh has a different view on this question. Several reports are attributed by Ḥanbalī scholars to Imam Ahmad ibn Ḥanbal. The first says that the woman's face is not part of the *'awrah*. The second makes a sweeping statement that the entire body of a woman is *'awrah*, but some scholars understand it to except her face or not to apply during prayer. A third report states that a woman may not uncover any part of her body during prayer, not even her nails. Lastly, it is reported that Imam Ahmad upheld 'Ā'ishah's afore-mentioned hadith: 'When a woman has attained puberty, it is not permissible that any part of her body be seen, except this and this, pointing to his face and hands.'

We need to call on the followers of the Ḥanbalī School to uphold 'Ā'ishah's hadith accepted by Imam Aḥmad, which was given added strength by al-Bayhaqī in old times and by Shaykh Nāṣir al-Albānī in recent days. They should also uphold the many hadith statements we mentioned in Chapter 3. Further, we call on them to give due importance to the fact that early scholars were all of the same view on this question. Their agreement was not due to any lack of knowledge of the Qur'an and the Sunnah, or the practice of the early blessed generations. Bearing all this in mind, we call on the followers of the Ḥanbalī School to acknowledge that the Muslim woman's face is not part of her *'awrah*. They should abandon other reports which are not based on any statement in the Qur'an or the Sunnah. They only rely on a statement by a companion of the Prophet and one of the *tābi'īn* explaining the meaning of a Qur'anic statement, which is differently explained by others.

Finally, let us carefully consider what Ibn al-Qayyim says about emulating scholars: 'A scholar may err; this is inevitable because he is not infallible. It is not right to accept all what he says, or to treat what he says as if it is said by the Prophet who is infallible. Such total following has been strongly criticized by every scholar on earth. They state that it is forbidden and they strongly criticize those who do it. It is, indeed, the undoing of those who emulate scholars, because they follow them in everything they say, whether right or wrong. Essentially, they cannot distinguish right from wrong. Thus, they consider a scholar's mistake a part of the religion, treating as permissible what God has made unlawful, legitimizing what He has forbidden and making laws He has not made. This is inevitable because the scholar they emulate is not infallible. Hence, he is bound to make some errors... Some may say that we acknowledge that the Imams who are emulated in religion follow right guidance. Therefore, those who emulate them are also following right guidance, because they follow in their footsteps. The answer is that following in their footsteps definitely makes them non-emulators. The method pursued by such Imams is to uphold the evidence and to censure blind following... A person who does not look at the evidence, commits what they have censured and what the Prophet prohibited does not follow their method. Indeed, his practice is contrary to what they approve of. Only a person who looks at the evidence and upholds the clear evidence follows their method. He must not take anyone other than the Prophet as a guide placing his words ahead of the Qur'an and the Sunnah... Al-Bayhaqī reports that Ibn 'Abbās said: 'Woe to the emulators from the slips of a scholar.' He was asked what he meant. He said: 'A scholar may say something according to his own view. He subsequently learns a hadith that is contrary to that view and he abandons that view, while his followers continue to follow what they had heard him say earlier.'

CHAPTER VI

The Veil, Prior to Islam and After It

In Pre-Islamic Days

The veil, i.e. *niqab* or *burqu'*, is mentioned by several poets who lived in pre-Islamic days, which confirms that it was known in Arabia before the advent of Islam. It was, then, one of the types of dress a woman used to wear. Islam neither enjoined nor prohibited wearing it. It left it to people and their traditions. It is well-known that Islam did not impose any particular style of clothing, leaving this to people so that they would choose what best suited their environmental and social conditions. The important thing is that the values Islam lays down should be heeded in any type or style Muslims choose to wear.

It may be said that the fact that the *niqab* was worn in pre-Islamic days does not lessen its status. The cloak, i.e. *jilbāb*, and the head covering, i.e. *khimār*, were also worn in pre-Islamic days. We know this for certain and we can quote pre-Islamic poetry that mentions both.

We, thus, have no disagreement that the *niqab*, cloak and head covering were worn in pre-Islamic days. However there is great difference between what was worn before Islam and confirmed by Islam, as Muslim women were ordered to use clothing in clear statements in the Qur'an and hadith, which included the cloak and head covering, and what Islam narrowed use of, disallowing the wearing of the *niqab* during consecration. Moreover, the great majority of female companions of the Prophet were not used to wearing the *niqab*, as we explained in Chapter 3.

It is true that Islam did not totally prohibit the *niqab*. Had it done so, it would have caused inconvenience to women who habitually used it, although they were few in the Muslim community. God says: 'He has laid no hardship on you in anything that pertains to religion.' (22: 78) In this respect, Islam left it open to wear the *niqab* in order to make it easier for some women to wear what they were used to. From another point of view, the *niqab* did not interfere with any interest of the Muslim community in the small societies where it was familiar. It had features that distinguished it from some contemporary types that deserve to be censured for the inconvenience and hardship they cause. Here are some good features that make the *niqab* more acceptable:

- That the *niqab* should not totally cover the woman's face, and as such it does not conceal her totally. It leaves room for recognition, particularly in small communities, like the old Bedouin communities, where people were small in number and they intermixed, making recognition of a woman easy despite her wearing the *niqab*.
- If the *niqab* allows recognition, it encourages women's participation in social life, as she continues to be able to communicate with her male relatives who are not *maḥram* to her. By contrast, a *niqab* that covers the face totally encourages isolating women from social life.

- If the *niqab* leaves the woman's eyes and their sockets visible, it enables her interlocutor to identify her feelings of pleasure or sorrow, content or discontent, acceptance or rejection.
- When the *niqab* does not cover the woman's eyes, it helps her to maintain her modesty. This applies particularly in the case of a woman whose weakness encourages her to look at all around her. The visibility of her eyes betrays her doing so, while if the *niqab* covers all her face, it is not easy to determine at whom or what she is looking.

The *Niqab* under Islam

Prohibiting the niqab *during consecration:*

- 'Abdullāh ibn 'Umar narrated: 'A man stood up and said: "Messenger of God, what clothes do you order us to wear during consecration?" The Prophet said: "Do not wear robes, trousers, turbans or cloaks with hoods. A man who does not have slippers may wear shoes but he should cut them below the ankles. Do not wear anything that has been perfumed with saffron or *warss*.[10] A woman who is in a state of consecration must not wear a veil or gloves."' (Related by al-Bukhari)

This hadith indicates that what is prohibited during consecration, whether for men or women, is every aspect of refined comfort and beautification. It calls for aspects of a rough life. In this connection, al-Bājī, the author of *al-Muntaqā Sharḥ al-Muwaṭṭa'*, says: 'A person in consecration is not allowed refinements... commanded to choose roughness.' This suggests that the *niqab* was a type of beautification and refinement some women used to wear, in the same mould of a

10. *Warss* is the name of a yellow plant with a pleasant smell, used as a dye.

turban, a hooded cloak and *khuffs* for men. All these types of clothing are stated in the same context in the hadith. Normally, types of clothing are not given a worshipful aspect, but are rather determined by personal preference and general custom. We should remember that this hadith about the restrictions for *iḥrām*, which took place at the time of the Prophet's Farewell Pilgrimage, is the only one in which the Prophet (peace be upon him) refers to *niqab*. This means that the *niqab* was not mentioned by him anywhere else in all the hadith anthologies we have perused.

Several considerations confirm that the *niqab* was a type of refined clothing, and these include:

a. While the *niqab* covers a part of the woman's face, it leaves another part, particularly the eyes uncovered. It may be that what it reveals is more beautiful than what it hides, particularly if the woman applies kohl to her eyes. This was women's common practice during the Prophet's lifetime. Subayʿah is said to have adorned herself when her postnatal condition was over. This is in a hadith related by al-Bukhari and Muslim. A different version related by Ahmad says that she 'applied kohl, henna and got herself ready'. Jābir narrates a long hadith describing the Prophet's hajj, and includes: ''Alī came from Yemen with the Prophet's camels, and he found that Fāṭimah had released herself from consecration. She wore a coloured dress and applied kohl.' (Related by Muslim)
b. Beautification may be by revealing or by covering: a man may wear nothing on his head and may comb his hair and give it a style. By contrast, to wear a turban, fez, hat or Arabian head covering is a type of beautification. The same applies to a woman: to uncover her face and apply some adornment, such as kohl, is beautification, and so is covering part of her face with a *niqab*. The *niqab* itself may be adorned to add to a woman's beautification.

c. Clothing differs from one environment to another according to climate, but it also differs within the same environment according to social classes. One type may be chosen by the elite, while another is worn by the general public and a third is distinctive of servants and others in their class. Was this the case in pre-Islamic Arabia? Men at the top of the social order used to wear upper and lower garments, or suits, while the poorer people were content to have lower garments. The same applied to women: those who belonged to the higher families were distinguished by their veils and wore cloaks. A poor woman, or a slave, wore basic clothes, uncovered her face and probably her head. This seemed to be an aspect of poverty while the *niqab* was an aspect of affluence. Does this remind us of the distinction made between free women and slaves in Muslim society at the time? Free women wore a cloak and head covering, while slaves walked about with no head covering. However, differences in types of clothing, including covering the woman's head or leaving it uncovered, with covering treated as an aspect of higher status and affluence while head exposure indicated low status, were not a special scenario in pre-Islamic or early Islamic days. This continued for many centuries. Muhammad Farīd Wajdī wrote early in the fourteenth Hijri century (twentieth century CE): 'It was generally accepted by women that covering indicates status and uncovering the practice of lower classes. Therefore, when a woman felt that she had risen in social status, through having some wealth, she immediately used the veil so as to be classed with free affluent women.'

A number of statements by some highly respected Fiqh scholars of the Ḥanbalī School confirm that the *niqab* was worn for beautification. The following are only a sample:

Abu al-Qāsim al-Khiraqī said: 'A wife whose husband has recently died must avoid perfume, adornments, staying overnight anywhere other than her own home, applying kohl and wearing the *niqab*.' He also said: 'A woman in mourning avoids wearing the *niqab*, because a woman in consecration refrains from wearing it. In this it is akin to perfume.'

Ibn Qudāmah said: 'What a woman in mourning should avoid includes the *niqab* and similar matters such as the *burqu'*, because she is in a similar position to one who is in consecration, or *iḥrām*.' Justice Abu Ya'lā said: 'Ahmad disapproved of *niqab* for a woman whose husband had recently died.'

However, Ibn al-Qayyim mentions in *Zād ak-Ma'ād*: 'Ibrāhīm ibn Hāni' al-Naysābūrī said in his questions: 'I asked Abu 'Abdullāh [i.e. Imam Ahmad] about a woman wearing the *niqab* during her waiting period. He said: "There is no harm in that."'

It appears as though two views are attributed to Imam Ahmad ibn Ḥanbal with regard to wearing the *niqab* by a woman in mourning. We have not quoted these views in order to state a definitive ruling on this question. We are merely interested in that they consider that a woman wearing the *niqab* is actually putting on some adornment, even though there are differences as to its extent. When we carefully look at the report permitting the wearing of the *niqab* by a woman in mourning, we note two points: First, the *niqab* has an element of adornment and it is controversial. This is the reason for putting the question in the first place. Had the *niqab* been associated only with decency and coverage, let alone coverage of *'awrah*, there would be no need to ask the question. Secondly, the answer is given in the form, "There is no harm in it." This states its permissibility, but not its desirability or obligation. Indeed, when a Fiqh scholar said about something that it involves no harm, he may mean that although it is not forbidden, it is better left out.

Having said all this, we conclude that the *niqab* was a type of clothing which some free women used to wear for beautification in pre-Islamic days. It continued to be so under Islam, as the Prophet (peace be upon him) approved of it, without recommending or urging its wearing. As we said earlier, had the *niqab* been considered a means of enhancing chastity and maintaining the woman's modesty, as some people claim, the Prophet (peace be upon him) would have chosen it for his wives who were the most entitled to these virtues. Moreover, the best of the Prophet's female companions would have chosen it, as they were keen to reflect these virtues. Yet, the Sunnah shows that neither the Prophet chose it for his wives nor did his female companions choose it for themselves. This is clear evidence that the *niqab* continued to be no more than a type of clothing some women chose for themselves. Subsequently, the Mothers of the Believers had their own distinctive status, requiring them to remain behind a screen inside their homes. When they went out, they still covered all their bodies, including their faces. We will discuss how this applies only to the Prophet's wives in Chapter 2 of Volume 5.

The *Niqab* in Islamic History

Foreword

We have chosen this heading for the following discussion, distinguishing it from the previous topic, 'The *niqab* under Islam,' because we do not have here clear and authentic texts to rely on in attributing our findings to Islam. The texts we have are ones with chains of transmission which we have proven to lack authenticity or we are unable to prove to be sound. As such, they are unsuitable as a basis for a religious ruling.

As we have said, the *niqab* was no more than a type of clothing some women used to wear in pre-Islamic days and after the advent of Islam. There is no religious statement to indicate its being a duty or desirable. There is merely an acknowledgement of its permissibility, deduced from the hadith that prohibits wearing it when a woman is in consecration. Under this topic, we wish to show some forms of historical application in a social study of this type of clothing: essentially asking the question, who used to wear it? The majority or merely a few? Why was it worn? When did women wear it and when did they discard it? Within such a study we propose to cite a few texts, despite the flaws attached to their chains of transmission. We do so because we treat these texts as mere historical statements that indicate the most important features of the *niqab* and the habits associated with it. We do so realizing that historical indications do not require the same high degree of authenticity as religious evidence.

ONE: WEARING THE NIQAB AND ITS IMPORT

Al-Bukhari mentions the following statement with an incomplete chain of transmission: 'Samurah ibn Jundab permitted a woman wearing the *niqab* to be a witness.' The report in this form mentions a specific case in which the woman was wearing the *niqab*. This indicates that the *niqab* was known at the time, but rarely used. This is the reason for the narrator stating it. Had covering women's faces been the norm, there would have been no need for the narrator to mention it, as most women would have worn the *niqab*. Moreover, had women generally been using the *niqab*, the statement would have been phrased differently, i.e. 'Samurah ibn Jundab permitted a woman to be a witness while wearing the *niqab*,' or 'He permitted women wearing the *niqab* to be witnesses.'

TWO: DISCARDING THE NIQAB AND ITS IMPORT

Facing a calamity

Qays ibn Shammās narrated: 'A woman called Umm Khallād came to the Prophet wearing a *niqab* and asking for information about her son who was killed. Some of the Prophet's companions said to her:

“Have you come to ask about your son and you are wearing a veil?” She said: “I may have the calamity of losing my son, but I shall not lose my modesty.” God’s Messenger said to her: “Your son shall have the reward of two martyrs.” She asked: “Why is it so, Messenger of God?” He said: ‘Because he was killed by people who follow earlier revelations.”’ (Related by Abu Dāwūd)

This hadith shows that the *niqab* was a type of clothing used by some people, not a cover required by religion. This is confirmed by the fact that it was also customary to take it off in some situations that called for avoiding refinement, such as sorrow for the loss of a loved one, as clearly appears in this hadith. The Prophet’s companions wondered at the woman wearing the *niqab* when she had lost her son. This continued to be the tradition in Muslim society, motivating leading Ḥanbalī scholars to say that a woman avoids wearing the *niqab* throughout the mourning period. The woman said: ‘I may have the calamity of losing my son, but I shall not lose my modesty.’ This does not suggest that women who did not wear the *niqab* were not modest. This is merely an expression of the feelings of a woman who is used to wearing it. She would have felt shy if she had taken it off, in the same way that a man who was used to wearing a head covering would feel shy without it, unless they are overcome by a feeling of grief or something similar.

The chain of transmission of this hadith is lacking in authenticity. Therefore, we do not use it as evidence for a religious ruling, but cite it only as a historical report indicating certain habits of women.

To identify oneself

‘Abdullāh ibn al-Zubayr narrated: ‘At the time when Makkah fell to Islam, Hind bint ‘Utbah and other women embraced Islam and they came to God’s Messenger (peace be upon him) when he was at al-Abṭaḥ [an open area in Makkah]. Hind said: “Messenger of God, all praise be to God who has given supremacy to the faith He has chosen. My relation to you will certainly benefit me. Muhammad, I am a woman who believes in God and His Messenger." She then removed her veil and said: "I am Hind bint 'Utbah." God's Messenger said: "You are welcome."' (Related by Ibn Sa'd in *al-Ṭabaqāt*)

This is again a historical statement indicating that a woman used to discard her *niqab*, without embarrassment, if she wished to identify herself. This confirms that the *niqab* covered the identity of the woman wearing it, to some extent, in addition to its being an article of refinement. It also confirms that wearing the *niqab* is not required by religion. Had it been a religious duty, the Prophet would have censured Hind bint 'Utbah for discarding it.

To warn of danger

The following story confirms what the previous two cases indicate: that discarding the *niqab* in some situations was a closely associated habit with its wearing. The story mentions that Laylā al-Akhyaliyyah's lover once found her without her *niqab* and felt the seriousness of the matter. She was asked: 'Why was he perturbed at you being without your *niqab*?' She said: 'He often used to come to see me. One day, he sent me a message that he would be coming. My people got wind of his coming and they sat in ambush. When he arrived, I uncovered my face, and he realized that it was a hint of impending danger. Therefore, he only greeted me and left.'

The story does not merely indicate that women discarded the *niqab* in some situations, but also indicates the nature of the *niqab* in those times: it was an article of refined clothing worn for beautification. Had the *niqab* been intended to cover the woman's face in the way that prevails in some Muslim countries where it is a thick veil covering the woman's whole face, Laylā al-Akhyaliyyah would have shed it when she met her lover away from the eyes of ill-wishers. She would also have increased her veiling at the moment of risk and danger.

But we see the opposite in this case. She is keen to wear the *niqab* at the time of private delight, because it implies beautification and refinement. She is also keen to discard it at the moment of danger, when beautification and refinement are not needed; rather, the need was for a clear warning.

We would not have discussed this last story at this length except for the fact that the habits associated with wearing the *niqab* and discarding it in some cases continued under Islam. We have seen how the Prophet's companions wondered at the woman who was enquiring about her martyred son wearing the *niqab*. We also saw that some Ḥanbalī scholars ordered the woman in mourning not to wear the *niqab*.

Concluding notes

Special features of the niqab

The *niqab* makes things a little easier for the woman, as it leaves her eyes uncovered and allows the sense of sight to operate without impediment. Thus, the woman sees people and things as they are, and the woman can enjoy the beauty of God's creation. God says: 'Say: "Who is there to forbid the beauty which God has produced for His servants, and the wholesome means of sustenance?"' (7: 32) Moreover, it allows easier operation of the resspiratory system.[11]

It covers a part of the woman's face and leaves another part uncovered. Thus, it makes it easy to recognize the woman wearing it. It shows some features of the woman's face so as to make it easier to recognize the woman when people meet again.

11. This can only be understood when we compare the *niqab* with its harsher version that covers the woman's face totally.

While it provides a gentle covering of a part of the woman's face, it also gently shows another part. While the cover is associated with modesty, the exposure is associated with beauty. The shown part may be prettier than the covered part, which means that the *niqab* may show the most beautiful part of the woman's face and cover the less beautiful. The shown part may make men more eager to see what is covered.

Islamic law is kinder to women

A man's *'awrah* extends over a limited part of his body. Therefore, there is scope to cover more than the *'awrah*, whether to protect oneself against hot or cold weather, or to ensure decent appearance. By contrast, the woman's *'awrah* extends over her entire body except her face, hands and feet. This means that there is no need for more coverage for protection or appearance. To add to what should be covered may constitute a burden and hardship, but God says: 'He has laid no hardship on you in anything that pertains to religion.' (22: 78) Yet there may be some hardship for the woman in having to cover all her body apart from her face, hands and feet in hot weather. We can only say that this is something God requires of women believers, and they should accept it with resignation. This measure of hardship is due to the nature of her body, which God has made pretty and tempting. It is totally unreasonable that Islam gives the woman a window to see the world around her, breathe fresh air and interact socially with people, but then close this window. Islam did not object to those women who were used to wearing the *niqab* as it was their social tradition. This is true, but neither did it encourage or urge it on others. It did not consider it desirable either. It left it as a matter of social custom which people may be happy with. Had it required them to discard it, they might have found this too hard.

Let us always remember that the *niqab* people used during the Prophet's lifetime, and was familiar to our grandfathers in Turkey and Egypt, and continues to be worn by Bedouins in Saudi Arabia, Egypt and other Gulf areas is of the gentler type. It covers only a part of the woman's face, leaving the eyes and the area around them visible. It does not prevent recognition and social interaction, particularly in small communities. The veil that some try to impose in some Muslim societies covers all the woman's face, impairs the sense of sight and the breathing function. It must be shunned if a woman finds it too hard. It cannot be said that it is a type of dress approved of by the Prophet. The Prophet approved the *niqab* which was familiar during his own lifetime, and which was a type of refined clothing worn for beautification. Had the Prophet seen the sort of face covering used today and realized how hard it is for women, we believe he would have disapproved of it and chosen what is easier for women. 'Ā'ishah, the Mother of the Believers, stated the truth: 'Whenever God's Messenger (peace be upon him) had to choose between two things, he would always choose the easier option.' (Related by Muslim)

Getting rid of the chains of tradition

It is a fact of human nature that getting rid of an established tradition is very hard. When something has been familiar for generations in a particular community, and they are comfortable with it, it has a hold on them that is very difficult to break. This is the case of the *niqab* in some Muslim countries. It was so in urban Egypt at the beginning of the fourteenth century of the Islamic Hijri calendar (twentieth century CE). An Egyptian poet describes the difficulty of breaking this particular tradition, saying:

> If we were to see Eve, our mother, walking in the streets of Egypt, holding the hand of the Virgin Mary, with their faces uncovered, and behind them Moses, Jesus, Muhammad and an army of kings, and they all tell us that it is permissible to discard the *niqab*, we will say: it is true, but we will keep it.

May God preserve us from the blind following of forefathers without proper guidance. May He enable us to always keep the Qur'an and the Sunnah as our guides. May we only emulate the Prophet's female companions who uncovered their faces in the presence of the Prophet and his male companions.

CHAPTER VII

Other Conditions of Women's Attire and Adornment[12]

CHAPTER SUMMARY:

- Condition 2: Moderate adornments of face, hands, feet and clothing
- Condition 3: Clothing and adornments must be socially acceptable.
- Condition 4: That in total, women's attire should be different from men's.
- Condition 5: That in total, women's attire and adornment must be different from what is distinctive of unbelievers.

12. Condition 1, which is covering all the woman's body except her face, hands and feet, was the subject of discussion in chapters 2-6 of the present volume.

Condition 2: *Moderate Adornments of Face, Hands, Feet and Clothing*

Foreword

Moderation is an essential feature of Islam. In adornment and other things, moderation is the opposite of excessiveness. Moreover, when adorning oneself, it is important to observe the tradition of believing women in every society, so that the adornment is not of the particularly eye-catching sort. There is no harm in that custom and tradition differ from one society to another, but what is important is moderation in all situations.

A Muslim woman should have a measure of apparent adornment throughout her life, whether she stays at home or goes out to participate in social life.

Apparent adornment includes henna or colour on a woman's hands, kohl applied to her eyes and a little makeup on her cheeks. The only time that she is exempt from such small measures of adornment is when she is in mourning for the death of a relative, which extends no more than three days except in the case of her husband when it extends for four months and ten days or until she gives birth if she happens to be pregnant when her husband dies. A Muslim woman must actually put on some adornment to indicate that she is no longer in mourning. This is what was done by two of the Prophet's wives: Umm Ḥabībah and Zaynab bint Jaḥsh, as well as Umm 'Aṭiyyah:

- Zaynab bint Abi Salamah said: 'When the news of Abu Sufyān's death arrived from Syria, Umm Ḥabībah called for yellow perfume on the third day and wiped with it the sides of her face and her cheeks. She said: 'I have no need for this except that I heard the Prophet (peace be upon him) say: "It is not lawful for a woman who believes in God and the Last Day to be in mourning for any deceased person more than three days, except for her husband: her mourning for him is four months and ten days."'' (Related by al-Bukhari and Muslim)
- Zaynab bint Abi Salamah narrated: '... I went into Zaynab bint Jaḥsh's home when her brother passed away. She called for some perfume and said: "I have no need for perfume but I heard the Prophet (peace be upon him) say: 'It is not lawful for a woman who believes in God and the Last Day to be in mourning for any deceased person more than three days, except for her husband: her mourning for him is four months and ten days.'"' (Related by al-Bukhari)
- Muhammad ibn Sīrīn narrated: 'A son of Umm 'Aṭiyyah passed away. On the third day, she called for yellow perfume and wiped herself. She said: "We have been commanded not to be in mourning for more than three days except for a husband."' (Related by al-Bukhari)

Keeping everything in moderation means that the woman continues with her ordinary life naturally, using her normal apparent adornments. This should be her appearance in most cases. She does not make a point of wearing special adornments when she intends to meet men or when men want to meet her. This is unbecoming of a woman believer who tries to avoid whatever invites temptation. She merely maintains her apparent adornments whether she stays at home or goes out, and whether her visitors are women or men.

A man seeks fine appearance by using a variety of clothes, because his *'awrah* is merely the genitals or the area between his waist line and his knees. As the woman's *'awrah* is all her body except her face, hands and feet, God gave her the added advantage of adornment to her face and hands, so that she may use kohl on her eyes and henna and colouring on her hands.

What appears of adornment naturally stays on for some time. The henna and colours may stay for months, while kohl stays for a few days. Other things like perfume mixed with saffron or other good-smelling colourings also linger for some time. These are of the type of women's makeup that shows its colour but where its smell disappears. This means that if a woman applies such adornment when she is at home, with her husband, children and other immediate relatives, then some other men come in, or she goes out to attend to some business, some men will inevitably see what appears of her adornment that she put on at home. All glory be to God, the Compassionate, the Ever-Merciful. He has placed no embarrassment on such a woman by requiring her to refrain from meeting men or to remove such adornment. He made an exception allowing its appearance, commanding women 'not to display their adornments except what may ordinarily appear thereof.' (24: 31)

That a Muslim woman wears some apparent adornments in most situations is a very natural tendency as God placed the love of adornment in the woman's nature right from her early childhood. God refers to girls as 'someone who is brought up among trinkets' (43: 18). Islam is consistent with human nature. Therefore, it requires or encourages men and women to stick to nature.

This natural tendency to wear adornments is emphasized as we note that one of the Prophet's companions expresses amazement when he sees his friend's wife having none of it. 'Awn ibn Abi Juḥayfah narrated from his father: 'The Prophet (peace be upon him) established a bond of brotherhood between Salmān and Abu al-Dardā'.[13] Salmān visited Abu al-Dardā' and he found Umm al-Dardā' wearing simple clothes. He asked her the reason and she said: "Your brother has no desire for anything in this life..." (Related by al-Bukhari)

The Islamic recommendation that women should wear their apparent adornments is further confirmed as the Mothers of the Believers wondered at the poor attire of a woman believer. This is further emphasized as the Prophet himself disapproved of her condition. Abu Mūsā al-Ash'arī narrated: "Uthmān ibn Maẓ'ūn's wife visited the Prophet's wives and they saw her in a poor condition. When the Prophet came in they mentioned this to him. He then met 'Uthmān and said to him: "'Uthmān, are you not required to follow my example..." She visited them later wearing adornments like a bride. They asked her: "How come?" She said: "We have experienced what other people have experienced."' (Related by al-Ṭabarānī)

'Ā'ishah, the Prophet's wife, narrated: 'Khawlah bint Ḥakīm, who was married to 'Uthmān ibn Maẓ'ūn, visited me. [The Prophet] noticed her poor attire. He said to me: "'Ā'ishah, how poor Khawlah appears!"' (Related by Ahmad)

Further, the application of a measure of apparent adornment in normal situations may be considered a duty. This order to have

---

13. The bond of brotherhood was meant to establish closer relations between the Prophet's Companions. The Prophet established it between totally unrelated Muslims. Salman was of Persian origin while Abu al-Dardā' belonged to the Khazraj tribe of the Anṣār.

such a measure attains maximum clarity when God's Messenger disapproves of a woman for not using some colouring. Ibn 'Abbās narrated that a woman came to the Prophet to give him her pledge of allegiance. She had not used any colouring. The Prophet did not accept her pledge until she had used some colouring. (Related by Abu Dāwūd)

'Ā'ishah narrated: 'A woman put out her hand to the Prophet to give him a paper, but the Prophet withheld his hand. She said: "Messenger of God, I put out my hand to give you a paper, but you did not take it". He said: "I did not know whether the hand belonged to a woman or a man." She said: "It is a woman's hand." He said: "If you are a woman, you would have changed the appearance of your fingers with henna."' (Related by al-Nasā'ī)

Adornment is something women need by nature. It is also a natural tendency required by the love of beauty which is inherent in human nature. A man seeks refinement as he wears fine clothes and a woman uses beautifying things such as kohl and henna, sometimes adding a *niqab*. The following hadith is very significant in this context: 'Abdullāh ibn Mas'ūd narrated: 'A man said to the Prophet: "Anyone of us loves to wear a fine robe and fine shoes." The Prophet said: "God is beautiful and He loves beauty."' (Related by Muslim)

We should reflect on the fact that God loves beauty for both men and women even when they are in a state of consecration, when roughness is required and applying perfume is prohibited. In order not to go too far so as to make people turn away from a person in consecration, Islam encourages wearing perfume before starting such consecration. 'Ā'ishah tells us about the Prophet's behaviour as he provides the model for people to follow. She said: 'I used to apply perfume to God's Messenger just before he entered into a state of consecration (in a different version related by Muslim: apply the best perfume), and also for his full release of consecration shortly before he performed the *ṭawāf [al-ifāḍah]* at the Ka'bah.' She also said: 'I can almost see the brightness of perfume on God's Messenger's forehead when he was in consecration...' (Related by al-Bukhari and Muslim)

'Ā'ishah also tells us about women's perfume: 'We used to go with the Prophet (peace be upon him) to Makkah. We would tie a perfumed bandage on our foreheads when we started consecration. If we sweat, [the perfume] would run down our faces. The Prophet would see this but he did not prohibit us [doing it].' (Related by Abu Dāwūd)

A lady companion of the Prophet also tells us about this: Umaymah bint Ruqayqah narrated that the Prophet's wives used head bandages which they had perfumed with *warss* and saffron, tying up the end of their hair to keep it away from their foreheads. They did this before they entered into consecration, and they would start their consecration in this way. (Related by al-Ṭabarānī)

May God bestow mercy on Imam al-Shāfi'ī, for he used to recommend that a woman should apply henna before she started her *iḥrām*. He said: 'I prefer that a woman should wear henna just before starting her consecration.' 'Abdullāh ibn 'Ubayd and 'Abdullāh ibn Dīnār reported that he said: 'It is a Sunnah that a woman should rub her hands with some henna and not start her consecration without it.'

We may finally say that adornment is a natural characteristic required by the relationship God has placed in the nature of man and woman. If she is a virgin, she wears her adornment to invite a marriage proposal. God's Messenger (peace be upon him) said: 'Had Usāmah been a girl, I would have given her fine clothes and adornment so as that she would be sought in marriage.' If she is a widow or a divorcee, she also adorns herself for a possible proposal. May God bestow mercy on Subay'ah al-Aslamiyyah: 'She was pregnant when her husband died... She gave birth soon after his death. When she finished her postnatal discharge, she adorned herself for a proposal.' (Related by al-Bukhari and Muslim) If she is married, she wears her apparent adornment for her husband, and adds her concealed adornment. God says the truth as he describes the best of women: 'The one who pleases him when he looks at her...' (Related by al-Nasā'ī)

The general evidence for the second condition

This is stated in the Qur'anic verse that says: 'Tell believing women... not to display their charms except what may ordinarily appear thereof.' (24: 31) In his commentary on this verse, al-Ṭabarī said: 'The more correct of all these views is the one that says it means "the face and two hands" because this includes kohl, rings, bracelets, henna and colouring.'

In his commentary on the Qur'an, al-Fakhr al-Rāzī said: 'Those who said that the 'charms' or 'adornments' in this verse refer to what is added to one's natural appearance sum it up under three headings, one of which is colouring such as kohl and colours: blackening to her eyebrows, saffron on her cheeks and henna on her hands and feet.'

We will now add further details from the Sunnah, speaking about each of these types of adornment.

One: Facial adornments

a. Women's makeup

Abu Hurayrah mentions that God's Messenger (peace be upon him) said: 'Men's makeup is what gives a strong smell, but no apparent colour, while women's makeup shows its colour but has no smell.'

‘Imrān ibn Ḥuṣayn narrated that the Prophet (peace be upon him) said: ‘... Men’s makeup is a smell with no colour, but women’s makeup is a colour without smell.’ Sa‘īd (one of the narrators) said: ‘They understood that his reference to women’s makeup speaks about a woman going out. If she is at home with her husband, she may put on whatever makeup she wants.’ (Related by Abu Dāwūd)

b. Types of facial makeup:

In *Fatḥ al-Bārī*, Imam Ibn Ḥajar says: ‘... Men’s makeup is not applied to their faces, which is the opposite of women’s makeup. It is women who apply makeup to their faces, adding to their adornment.’ In *al-Mu‘jam al-wasīṭ*, the word *khumrah* is defined as ‘a mixture of makeup products which a woman applies to her face to improve her colour’. Anas ibn Mālik narrated that ‘Abd al-Raḥmān ibn ‘Awf came to see the Prophet and there were traces of saffron on him. God’s Messenger asked him about it and he told him that he married an Anṣārī woman. (Related by al-Bukhari and Muslim)

That the bride in this case used saffron in such a way that its traces were seen on the bridegroom, ‘Abd al-Raḥmān ibn ‘Awf, gives a strong suggestion that Abu Usayd al-Sā‘idī’s wife and also al-Rubayyi‘ bint Mu‘awwidh – whom we will be mentioning – still had traces of their bridal makeup when they met men:

- Sahl narrated: ‘When Abu Usayd al-Sā‘idī got married, he invited the Prophet and his companions. The one who cooked the food and served it to them was none other than his wife, Umm Usayd.’ In another version: ‘It was his wife, the bride, who served them on that occasion.’ (Related by al-Bukhari and Muslim)
- Khālid ibn Dhakwān narrated from al-Rubayyi‘ bint Mu‘awwidh; she said: ‘The Prophet visited me the morning after my wedding and he sat on my bed as you are seated now. We had maids playing on the tambourine, praising my

ancestors who were killed in the Battle of Badr.' (Related by al-Bukhari)

- Umm Salamah narrated: 'When a woman gave birth during the lifetime of God's Messenger (peace be upon him), she rested for forty days. We used to apply *warss* on our faces because of the rash we had.. (Related by al-Tirmidhī)
- 'Ā'ishah, the Prophet's wife narrated: ''Uthmān ibn Maẓ'ūn's wife used to wear henna and makeup, but then she abandoned that. She visited me once, and I asked her whether her husband was in town or away. She said: "It is the same if he is here or away." I asked her: What is the matter with you? She said: "'Uthmān wants nothing of this life and does not want women."' (Related by Ahmad)

In the Foreword to this chapter, we mentioned the hadith in which 'Umm Ḥabībah called for yellow perfume on the third day and wiped with it the sides of her face and her cheeks'. 'Ā'ishah also narrated: 'We used to apply musk to our faces before we entered into a state of consecration, then we started *iḥrām*.'

To emphasize the difference between the adornments of women and those of men, the Prophet used to censure any man who used female adornments. Here are some examples:

- Anas narrated: 'A group of people came to pledge allegiance to the Prophet, and one of them had traces of saffron mixed with perfume on his hand. The Prophet accepted their pledges but he kept delaying this man. He then said: 'Men's adornment gives smell and shows no colour, but women's adornment shows colour and gives no smell.' (Related by al-Bazzār)
- 'Alī ibn Abi Ṭālib narrated: 'The Prophet passed by a group of people among whom was one who showed some adornment. The Prophet greeted them but did not greet that man. He

said: "Messenger of God, you greeted them and turned away from me." The Prophet said: "You have red colouring in between your eyes."' (Related by al-Ṭabarānī)

- 'Ammār ibn Yāsir narrated: 'I came to my family one night with cuts on my hands. They applied saffron to my hands. In the morning, I went to the Prophet and greeted him. He did not reply and did not welcome me. He [only] said: "Go and wash this off."' (Related by Abu Dāwūd)

c. Kohl on the eyes:

There are several hadiths that show that female companions of the Prophet used to apply kohl, and this was merely for good appearance, not as medication. This was certainly their normal practice, and it was part of their standard makeup.

- Umm 'Aṭiyyah said: 'We were commanded not to remain in mourning for anyone more than three days, except for a husband: four months and ten days during which we must not wear kohl, perfume or any colourful dress.' (Related by al-Bukhari and Muslim)
- Subay'ah's case: '... When she finished her postnatal period, she adorned herself, hoping for a marriage proposal. Abu al-Sanābil came into her home... He said to her: "How come you are adorning yourself [hoping] for a proposal..."' (Related by al-Bukhari and Muslim) A different version narrated by Ahmad: 'Abu al-Sanaābil met her... when she had worn kohl, used colouring [makeup] and made herself ready.'
- Jābir narrated: ''Alī came from Yemen with the Prophet's camels, and he found that Fāṭimah had released herself from consecration. She wore a coloured dress and applied kohl. He censured her for that. She said: My father ordered me to do it'. (Related by Muslim)
- Umm Salamah narrated: 'God's Messenger (peace be upon him) visited me when Abu Salamah passed away. I had applied

aloe vera drops to my eye. He asked me: "What is this, Umm Salamah?" I said: "It is aloe vera; it has no perfume." He said: "It makes the face radiant. Therefore, apply it only at night."' (Related by al-Nasā'ī)

Two: Hand adornment

a. Colouring: We have quoted on several occasions the hadith stating the case of Subay'ah which mentions that she applied kohl, colour makeup and prepared herself. We also mentioned the hadith narrated by Ibn 'Abbās stating that, 'A woman came to the Prophet to pledge her allegiance. She had no hand colouring, and the Prophet did not accept her pledge until she had adorned her hands. We also quoted the hadith narrated by 'Ā'ishah in which the Prophet said to one woman: 'Had you been [truly] a woman you would have changed [the appearance] of your hands with henna.'"

   We may also add the following hadith but we are only citing it as a historical, not religious evidence because of the weakness of its chain of transmission: 'Mu'ādhah mentions that a woman asked 'Ā'ishah: "May a woman use colour makeup during her period?" 'Ā'ishah said: "We lived in the Prophet's home and used colour makeup, but he did not forbid us."' (Related by Ibn Mājah)

b. Rings: The Prophet's female companions used to wear rings, earrings and other articles of jewellery. Ibn 'Abbās narrated: 'God's Messenger (peace be upon him) went down and Bilāl was with him. He thought that his voice did not reach the women. He [addressed and] admonished them, encouraging them to donate to charity [i.e. *ṣadaqah*]. Women threw their earrings and rings, and Bilāl collected these in his robe.' (Related by al-Bukhari and Muslim)

c. Bracelets: Asmā' bint Yazīd narrated: 'I entered the Prophet's home with my maternal aunt and we were wearing gold bracelets. He said: "Do you pay its zakat?" We said: "No." He said: "Do you not fear that God may give you bracelets of fire? Pay its zakat."' (Related by Ahmad)

Three: Feet adornment

A number of statements refer to adornment which is worn on a woman's feet. These include:

- In reference to 'what may ordinarily appear' of adornment, 'Ā'ishah said: '*Fatakh* refers to rings of silver that are worn on toes.'
- Al-Fakhr al-Rāzī said: 'Scholars who said that adornments refer to things that are added to how a person is created classify these under three headings, one of which is ... henna worn on a woman's hands and feet.'
- Al-Shawkānī and Ṣiddīq Ḥasan Khān said: 'You are well aware that the apparent meaning of the Qur'anic text prohibits displaying adornments except what appears of it normally, such as a cloak, or a ring and similar articles of jewellery or similar matters that are worn on one's hands and feet.'

Four: Clothing

A number of hadiths speak of clothing as adornments, such as the one narrated by Anas ibn Mālik saying that he 'saw Umm Kulthūm, the Prophet's daughter, wearing a fine cloak adorned with silk.'

'Abdullāh ibn 'Umar narrated: '... God's Messenger was sent a number of suits adorned with silk. He sent one to 'Umar, one to Usāmah ibn Zayd and gave one to 'Alī ibn Abi Ṭālib telling him: "Cut it into head coverings for your women." (Another version related by al-Ṭabarānī: 'for the Fāṭimahs.') 'Umar came [to the Prophet] carrying his suit.

He said: "Messenger of God, you sent me this and you said yesterday whatever you said regarding the 'Uṭārid's suit!" The Prophet said: "I did not send it for you to wear, but to get some gain through it." Usāmah came in the morning wearing his suit, and God's Messenger stared at him. He realized that the Prophet disliked what he did. He said: "Messenger of God, why are you looking at me like this when it was you who sent it to me?" The Prophet said: "I did not send it to you so that you wear it, but to cut it into head coverings for your women."' (Related by Muslim)

The Fāṭimahs mentioned in this hadith are: Fāṭimah the Prophet's daughter, Fāṭimah bint Asad who was 'Alī's mother, and Fāṭimah bint Ḥamzah ibn 'Abd al-Muṭṭalib.

'Ikrimah narrated that Rifā'ah divorced his wife, and she got married to 'Abd al-Raḥmān ibn al-Zabīr al-Quraẓī. 'Ā'ishah said: 'She was wearing a green head cover. She put her complaint to her and showed her that her skin was getting green. When the Prophet came in – and women stand by women – 'Ā'ishah said: "I have not seen anything like what women suffer. Her skin was greener than her garment."' (Related by al-Bukhari.)

Islam does not specify any particular colour for the clothes of either men or women, which means that any colour is permissible. What constitutes 'moderate adornment' in clothing is subject to social norms in any particular area. It is common knowledge in all generations that certain colours and adornments may prevail among women believers and are acceptable to scholars in a particular country or province but may be questionable or even unacceptable in another. Colour and style may differ from one country to another, and they may also differ in the same country from one generation to another. Imam al-Ṭabarī states the truth as he says: 'To observe the prevailing style of clothing is an aspect of decency, unless the style itself is sinful. To go against it is to seek public attention.'

Moderation in the sort of adornment added to clothing ensures that they are not eye-catching or revealing. To be revealing means that a woman shows of her charms and adornments what is particularly appealing to men. If clothes are beautiful but not sharp in colour, and of fine but not head-turning style, and if these colours and styles are well-known and used by Muslim women, they are not considered 'inviting' to men. This means that neither by the woman's intention nor by the actual effect, the very idea of arousing men's desire is entertained, because such colourful and multi-style clothes are familiar to men and often used by women. This is the case in some Muslim countries. The multiple colours with the same style are found in the Sudanese top dress and the outer garment of rural Syrian women. Multiplicity of colour and style are seen among religious women students in Egyptian and Kuwaiti universities. The majority of such students wear different colours and styles, yet they maintain an attitude of religious decorum and are treated with clear respect.

A word of comment on adornment

Decent attire and appearance differ from time to time and place to place. Women in Arabia during the Prophet's lifetime considered henna on their hands, kohl on their eyes and yellow face colouring becoming to a woman's appearance. As we have noted, the Prophet not only mentioned this, but even encouraged it on occasions. This does not mean that these items in particular are permissible. They are examples that may be comparable to others, provided that the conditions we mentioned are observed. Social norms may change and red colour applied to the face may replace yellowness in some societies or some periods.

Ibn Qudāmah of the Ḥanbalī School said: 'It is forbidden for a woman in mourning to darken her face with Kalkoon, or whiten it with the Isfidaj which are used by brides, because these are more of adornment than henna.' [Kalkoon was a stuff used by women to give one's face a tinge of redness while Isfidaj was a white stuff used especially by brides.]

Ibn al-Qayyim said: 'She is forbidden to adorn herself with henna and other colours, paint her hands, use reddening and Isfidaj. The Prophet mentioned henna in particular to alert to all such matters that are more of adornment.'

Frequently asked questions about women's adornment

Having mentioned all this evidence from the Qur'an and the Sunnah about the legitimacy of moderate adornment applied to a woman's face, hands, feet and clothes, we would like to address some questions and objections that are often raised concerning wearing any adornment or makeup when women meet men.

1. PEOPLE SAY THAT A WOMAN'S FACE IS ITSELF CHARMING. IS IT RIGHT TO ADD TO ITS CHARM BY THE APPLICATION OF ADORNMENTS?

Several points may be stated in answer. This is not a question that we determine according to our own reasoning. It is a matter for religious text, or texts. If the Legislator approves of such adornment, no one may object to what He has legislated.

The Islamic attitude to the temptation caused by women's adornment is the same as its attitude to the temptation presented by women generally. It clearly states that there is temptation associated with women. Indeed, it is the strongest temptation. Yet it does not stop women from playing their role in all areas of society and meeting with men. It states certain rules of propriety that a woman must observe as she plays her role. There are such rules for conversation, walking and meeting. When these rules of propriety and decorum are observed, temptation is kept in check in all general situations. The same applies to adornment. Islam does not prohibit it, but it puts in place rules of propriety. These are: (1) it is colour without strong smell, as the hadith says: 'Women's adornment is what shows its colour but not its smell;' (2) it is kept in moderation, not eye-turning. This is based on the fact that the Legislator has approved rings and colour or henna as hand adornment and kohl and yellow colouring as face adornment; (3) that it is something that meets general agreement among Muslim women. This is based on the hadith that says: 'Whoever wears a garment that attracts people's gazes shall be made by God to wear a garment of humiliation on the Day of Judgement;' and (4) that the woman must not intend her adornment to stir men's desire. This is based on the Qur'anic verse that says: 'Do not display your charms as [women] used to display them in the old days of pagan ignorance.' (33: 33) When this code of manners is observed, temptation is kept well in check. We need not add anything further and be more strict in order to address our own delusions.

2. PEOPLE SAY THAT THERE ARE MANY TEXTS THAT WARN AGAINST WOMEN GOING OUT WEARING PERFUME

Again we have several points to make. We will start by stating a number of texts that warn against wearing perfume when a woman is about to go out, and we will then discuss their import.

- Zaynab al-Thaqafiyyah used to narrate that God's Messenger (peace be upon him) said: 'If any woman of you attends the 'Ishā' Prayer, she should not wear perfume on that night.' (Related by Muslim)
- Zaynab, 'Abdullāh's wife, said: 'God's Messenger (peace be upon him) said to us: "If any of you is attending the mosque, she should not wear perfume."' (Related by Muslim)
- Abu Hurayrah narrated that God's Messenger (peace be upon him) said: 'Any woman who has applied incense should not attend the 'Ishā' Prayer with us.' (Related by Muslim)
- Abu Hurayrah narrated that God's Messenger (peace be upon him) said: 'Do not prevent God's women servants from attending God's mosques, but they should go out wearing no perfume.' (Related by Abu Dāwūd)

ଓ Abu Hurayrah narrated that he met a woman whose perfume was still strong-smelling... He said: 'Servant of the Almighty, have you been to the mosque?' She said: 'Yes.' He said: 'And you have used perfume for going there?' She said: 'Yes.' He said: 'I heard my beloved one, Abu al-Qāsim (peace be upon him), say: "The prayer of a woman who wears perfume to come to this mosque shall not be accepted until she has gone back and taken a bath in the same way as she removes ceremonial impurity."' (Related by Abu Dāwūd)

It should be noted that all these hadiths speak about going to the mosque. A mosque has a special status which does not apply to other places. This is due to the fact that it is attended by a group of women who stand in rows that are close together, behind the rows of men. The two groups are close to each other, with no barrier between them. This may make the smell of perfume very strong and cause the scent to spread far. Ibn Qudamah mentions the hadith narrated by 'Ā'ishah: 'We used to come out with God's Messenger (peace be upon him) and we would apply musk on our foreheads. If any of us sweat, the musk would run down her face. The Prophet might see us and he would not object.' Ibn Qudāmah adds that 'This applies equally to young and older women. If someone asks: is that not stated to be reprehensible at Friday Prayer? We will say: it is so because at Friday Prayer, women are closer to men and the fear of temptation becomes stronger.'

Apart from the fact of the closeness of the women's and men's rows in the mosque, prayer requires focused attention so that a person is totally devoted to addressing God. Therefore, women are not allowed to glorify God aloud in a congregational prayer when they feel that something is amiss. Yet such glorification is no more than two words, while God allows women to speak to men decently, even at length. This means that in situations other than prayer, men hear women's voices normally, without restriction, even in a long conversation.

This, then, concerns going out to the mosque, while if a woman goes anywhere else, adorning herself in a way that shows its colour but not its smell – which is a condition in women's adornments – there is nothing she can spread to stir temptation.

A different hadith is narrated by Abu Mūsā al-Ash'arī who said that God's Messenger (peace be upon him) said: 'If a woman wears perfume and passes by some people so that they would smell her, then she is so-and-so.' He said that the Prophet added something very strong. (Related by Abu Dāwūd)

We note that the hadith mentions two points on which the woman contravenes the limits drawn by the Islamic code of conduct. The first is that she 'wears perfume' which means that she applied to herself perfume that clearly imparts a scent, and the other is that she passes by people 'so that they would smell her'. This means that she intentionally stirred temptation. Hence, she deserved this strong censure. What we have established, on the basis of texts, is that a woman may wear adornment within the limits established by God, the Legislator.

In summary, three things are prohibited when we speak about women's adornment: (1) attending congregational prayer in the mosque when she has applied perfume; (2) going out having applied perfume with clear scent; and (3) displaying charms in order to excite men's desire. If these three prohibitions are avoided, there is no harm if a woman wishes to adorn herself with something that gives fine colour but no smell.

3. PEOPLE SAY: WE UNDERSTAND THAT A WOMAN SHOULD ADORN HERSELF WHEN SHE IS WITH HER HUSBAND BECAUSE OF THE NATURE OF THE RELATIONSHIP BETWEEN MAN AND WIFE. WHAT, THEN, JUSTIFIES HER ADORNING HERSELF FOR MEN GENERALLY?

Again, our answer states more than one point. Adornment that is displayed before a woman's husband and her immediate male relatives whom she cannot marry is the inner adornment, which is referred to in God's words: 'Let them... not display their charms to any but their husbands, or their fathers, or their...' (24: 31)

What we have been talking about is the type of adornment that appears in the ordinary way, which is the adornment on a woman's face, hands and clothing. This is what is referred to in the same verse as adornment that 'may ordinarily appear'.

That a married woman adorns herself for her husband does not mean that an unmarried woman may not adorn herself at all. Wearing adornments is certainly more needed by married women so as to make it desirable, or even a duty, while in the case of an unmarried woman it is permissible, or even desirable, according to what interest is served by such adornment. That a Muslim, man and woman, appears in a fine style and moderate adornment is appreciated in an Islamic society that heeds the Prophet's statement: 'God is beautiful and loves beauty.' As we mentioned in the Foreword to this chapter, married women wear adornments primarily for the sake of their husbands. Unmarried women adorn themselves so that they are noticed by those who wish to be married. This is evidenced by the Qur'anic verse that includes: 'When they have reached the end of their waiting-term, you shall incur no sin in whatever they may do with themselves in a lawful manner'. (2: 234) In *al-Jalālayn* commentary on the Qur'an, 'Whatever they may do with themselves,' is explained as wearing adornments and showing themselves to those seeking marriage. Also in the Foreword, we mentioned the hadith that says: 'Had Usāmah been a girl, I would have given her fine clothes and adornment so as that she would be sought in marriage.' We also noted the hadith concerning Subay'ah: 'When she finished her postnatal discharge, she adorned herself for a proposal.'

There is a gulf of difference between a woman adorning herself in the hope of receiving a marriage proposal and one who adorns herself to please irreligious people. Those who are seeking marriage love beauty, but they prefer a woman who is modest and careful of her chastity to be their life partner and their children's mother. In addition, a God-fearing woman who hopes for a marriage proposal will definitely observe Islamic manners. The one who wants to please irreligious people will definitely be excessive in her adornment and will not abide by good believers' dress code.

4. PEOPLE SAY: WE UNDERSTAND THAT A WOMAN WHO WANTS TO GET MARRIED WISHES TO ADORN HERSELF IN THE HOPE OF A PROPOSAL, BUT WHAT ABOUT ONE WHO DOES NOT WISH TO GET MARRIED?

To start with, women who do not wish to get married are rare in a Muslim society. Normally, women in a Muslim society are either married or hopeful of marriage. This is motivated by the very nature of Muslim society where chastity and maintaining it are essential values. This is also encouraged by the Prophet's statement that marriage is part of his Sunnah. He also said: 'Whoever turns away from my Sunnah does not belong to me.' In reference to marriage, he said: 'It helps to lower one's gaze and maintain chastity.'

We may also add a reminder of what we said earlier that Muslims, men and women, whether married or not, wish to be married or wish to remain single, should always maintain a fine appearance and moderate adornment. This is characteristic of Islamic society.

5. PEOPLE SAY: WOMEN'S ADORNMENT IN WESTERN SOCIETY HAS BECOME VERY EXCESSIVE. UNFORTUNATELY, SOME MUSLIM SOCIETIES ARE BLINDLY FOLLOWING IN THEIR FOOTSTEPS IN MANY EXTERNAL ASPECTS INCLUDING WEARING EXCESSIVE ADORNMENTS. IS THERE ANY WAY TO GUARANTEE THAT A MODERN MUSLIM WOMAN WHO WANTS TO ADORN HERSELF WILL BE SPARED THIS UNBECOMING EMULATION?

Muslim women in all generations and communities have their own good role model, which is the 'Muslim woman during the Prophet's lifetime'. This applies to the general line of action drawn by Islam, not to the different ways of implementation governed by local conditions. In this, a Muslim woman who seeks to earn God's pleasure on the one hand and success and advancement on the other has a perfect role model.

Blind following, in any direction, adversely affects man's mind and heart. Every wise person steers away from becoming a prey of blind following. In every life issue, a Muslim considers and studies, looking first for divine guidance in the Qur'an and the Sunnah, and considering next the Muslim community's experience across generations, and finally studying other communities modern experience in particular. We should continue to study our own situations in order to ultimately arrive at what is right and proper, and then follow it with care and enlightenment.

Finally, a Muslim woman who wishes to obey God and follow the guidance of Muhammad (peace be upon him) realizes that emulating the West means discarding two essential conditions of wearing adornments, namely, moderation and general acceptability by Muslim women.

What scholars say about women's apparent adornment

In *al-Muwaṭṭa'*, Imam Mālik says: 'A man or a woman who is in *i'tikāf* may apply makeup and adornment.' This means that even when a woman is staying in a mosque for worship, she is not deprived of her adornment which shows its colour but not its smell. This is an aspect of proper appearance.

In *al-Umm*, Imam al-Shāfi'ī writes: 'Sa'īd reported from Mūsā ibn 'Ubaydah, from his brother 'Abdullāh ibn 'Ubaydah and 'Abdullāh ibn Dīnār; both said: "It is part of the Sunnah that as she is about to start her *iḥrām* or consecration, a Muslim woman should wipe her hands with some henna, rather than start without it." Al-Shāfi'ī said: This is what I would like for her. He also said: If a woman in *iḥrām* applies henna to her hands wrapping them, she should pay an indemnity, but if she merely wipes her hands with henna, I do not think that an indemnity becomes due, but I dislike this for her because it is the start of adornment. He further said: Sa'īd ibn Sālim reported from Ibn Jurayj that some people asked him about using perfume-free antimony kohl[14] by a woman in consecration. He said: "I dislike it, because it is adornment, and the days of consecration are days of humility and worship."'

These statements show that there is no restriction preventing a woman from wearing kohl, henna or colour adornment in general situations, but it is not appropriate when she is in consecration. In fact there is some emphasis on the fact that it is proper for a woman to apply some henna before starting her consecration.

A leading Ḥanafī scholar, al-Sarakhsī said: 'A woman in consecration may wear silk and jewellery during her consecration. The correct view is that it is acceptable. It has been reported that Ibn 'Umar used to allow his women to wear jewellery during consecration. God's Messenger (peace be upon him) saw two women performing the *ṭawāf* at the Ka'bah, wearing two gold bracelets... This hadith shows that it is acceptable.'

Ibn Qudāmah, a distinguished scholar of the Ḥanbalī School, said: 'To take a bath, wear some adornment and cleanse oneself just before entering into consecration is desirable for both man and woman. We have already cited the hadith narrated by 'Ā'ishah: "We used to come out with God's Messenger (peace be upon him) and we would apply musk on our foreheads. If any of us sweat, the musk would run down her face. The Prophet might see us and he would not object. This applies equally to young and older women."'

14. A type of kohl which is silvery coloured.

In *Mawāhib al-Jalīl li-Sharḥ Mukhtaṣar Khalīl*, al-Ḥaṭṭāb, a distinguished Mālikī scholar said: 'In Ibn al-Ḥāj's *Manāsik* we read: "There is no harm in a woman performing the *ṭawāf* wearing jewellery." It is reported that the Prophet saw a woman performing the *ṭawāf* at the Ka'bah, wearing gold jewellery with precious stones. He said to her: "Will you be pleased if God gives you similar ornaments made of fire?" She said: "No." He said: "Then pay its zakat." We note that the Prophet did not forbid her wearing such jewellery.' He wanted her to pay its zakat.

Ibn Baṭṭāl, a distinguished scholar who wrote a full commentary on al-Bukhari's *Ṣaḥīḥ*, which is published in eleven volumes, said: 'The hadith narrated by 'Ā'ishah states: "I used to apply the best perfume I could find to God's Messenger, until I could see the brightness of the perfume on his head and beard.' This hadith shows that men's makeup is not applied on their faces, which is the opposite of women's makeup. Women apply it to their faces and it is part of their adornment. In contrast, a man should not apply makeup on his face because he is commanded not to imitate women.'

This clearly shows that during the time of the Prophet, when a Muslim woman applied some of her makeup, its effect remained on her face and was seen by men who were not her immediate relatives. It was part of the apparent adornment which was seen by all and did not stir temptation because it had no noticeable smell.

Imam Ibn Ḥajar said: 'The distinction between the makeup of men and women is that women are commanded to be well covered when they leave home. Had she been allowed to apply makeup that gives off a pleasant smell, it would add to the temptation.'

Justice Ibn Rushd said: 'According to Fiqh scholars generally, a woman in mourning abandons adornment that attracts men to women, such as jewellery and kohl... Generally speaking, scholars' statements concerning what a woman in mourning should avoid are very close, referring to what attract men to her... Scholars who say that mourning applies only to a widow, and not to a divorcee, confine themselves to the apparent meaning of the stated text... The ones who apply it to divorcees during their waiting period rely on the meaning. It appears from the meaning of *iḥdād*, which is translated as 'mourning', that it is the aim that during her waiting period, neither men see her as attractive nor is she attracted to them. This is a case of preventing the cause leading to an undesirable development. The ultimate purpose is to preserve correct parenthood, but God knows best.'

What Justice Ibn Rushd says implies that unrelated men normally see the apparent adornment of a woman, such as her kohl and jewellery. She is not allowed to wear such adornment during her waiting period so that men do not see her well adorned and find her desirable as she herself may desire them. Along the same lines, Ibn al-Qayyim says in *Zād al-Ma'ād*: 'The hadith that says, "A woman may not be in mourning for anyone more than three days, except for her husband," suggests distinction between the two forms of mourning in two ways: status and duration. To be in mourning for a deceased husband is a duty to be undertaken with resolve, while for anyone else it is permissible as a concession... Sa'īd ibn al-Musayyib, Abu 'Ubayd, Abu Thawr, Abu Ḥanīfah and his disciples, as well as Imam Ahmad in his reported view chosen by al-Khiraqī said: "An irrevocably divorced woman must observe mourning... because she is observing a waiting period after the termination of her marriage. Hence, she needs to be in mourning like one who is widowed... Since the waiting period prohibits making a marriage contract, it also prohibits its causes..." They also said: "Undoubtedly, mourning is logically understood to prevent showing adornment, makeup and jewellery that increases a woman's appeal to men and their appeal to her..."'

Condition 3: Clothing and Adornments Must Be Socially Acceptable

The evidence confirming this condition is the hadith quoting the Prophet (peace be upon him): 'Whoever wears a garment that attracts people's gazes shall be made by God to wear a garment of humiliation on the Day of Judgement and then He will set it on fire.' (Related by Abu Dāwūd)

The hadith refers to a person who wears clothes that are considered odd in his Muslim community, with the purpose of attracting other people's attention to himself so that he becomes well known. He is not the same as the one who wears something that is different from his usual clothes, but does not intend this for personal publicity but rather has some motive that serves a particular interest. Observing what is generally acceptable is desirable and a Muslim should always attend to this. However, if a good reason or a need requires a person to wear something that is different from what is familiar to people, there is no harm. Going against what is traditionally acceptable is seen as permissible in proportion to the interest or need it serves. We may repeat here what Imam al-Ṭabarī said: 'To observe the prevailing style of clothing is an aspect of decency, unless it is sinful. To go against it is to seek public attention.'

Social tradition that should be respected is what is consistent with Islamic laws and values. If it is not, then it deserves neither respect nor attention. A society may become accustomed to extravagance in matters of clothing and other areas. An advocate of Islam or a reformer may need to practically go against what is familiar to people because it is better for them and more consistent with their faith.

Condition 4:
That in Total, Women's Attire Should Be Different from Men's

The evidence is provided by the following hadiths:

- Ibn 'Abbās narrated: 'God's Messenger (peace be upon him) cursed men who imitate women and women who imitate men.' (Related by al-Bukhari)
- Abu Hurayrah narrated: 'God's Messenger (peace be upon him) cursed the man who wears a woman's attire and the woman who wears a man's attire.' (Related by Abu Dāwūd)

These hadiths disapprove of imitation generally, in clothing and other ways. However, in matters of dress, it does not prohibit that a piece of a woman's clothing may be similar to men's clothes. The point here is concerned with the general attire, so that when a Muslim woman is seen - even at a distance - her appearance is not that of a man. However, the prohibition applies even to a single piece, if it is socially recognized to belong to men only. This means that social standards are given great importance.

To prove that the purpose here is the prohibition of similarity as applied to general appearance, not the common usage of a particular piece of clothing, we may quote the following hadiths:

- Sahl ibn Sa'd reports that 'A woman came to the Prophet and said: "Messenger of God! I have come to make of myself a present to you." The Prophet looked her up and down several times, then he lowered his head. When the woman realized that the Prophet did not make a decision concerning her offer, she sat down. One of his companions said: "Messenger of God, if you have no need of her, give her to me in marriage." The Prophet asked him: "Do you have something to give her?" He said: "No, Messenger of God... but here is my lower garment. She may have half of it." The Prophet said: "What good is your lower garment to her? If you wear it, she has nothing of it, and if she wears it, you will have nothing of it..."' (Related by al-Bukhari and Muslim)
- Usāmah ibn Zayd narrated: 'God's Messenger (peace be upon him) gifted me a thin opaque white garment which was part of what Diḥyah al-Kalbī had gifted him. I gave it to my wife to wear. God's Messenger asked me why I had not worn it. I told him that I gave it to my wife. He said: "Tell her to wear a vest under it, as I fear that it may describe the size of her bones."' (Related by Ahmad and al-Ṭabarānī)
- Asmā' bint Abu Bakr said: 'The sun was eclipsed during the Prophet's lifetime and I heard people's disturbance as they said: "A miracle"... I went out drawing over myself a shawl belonging to al-Zubayr. I entered 'Ā'ishah's place while the Prophet was leading people in prayer...' (Related by Ahmad)

Explaining the hadith narrated by ibn 'Abbās which curses men imitating women in their appearance, Ibn Ḥajar said: 'Clothing fashions differ from one area to another. In a certain community, women's clothes may be similar to men's clothes, but women are distinguished by their head covers and covering all their bodies.' Covering may be by wearing a certain type of head cover or a cloak.

Ibn Taymiyyah said: 'If a certain article of clothing is worn mostly by men, women are told not to wear it, even though it may provide full covering of their bodies, such as the *farajiyyah*, which is a wide robe with long sleeves worn by scholars in certain places. Prohibition of wearing such garments may change as habits and traditions change.'

Condition 5: That in Total, Women's Attire and Adornment Must Be Different from What is Distinctive of Unbelievers

The evidence confirming this condition is provided by the following hadiths:

- 'Abdullāh ibn 'Amr ibn al-'Āṣ narrated: 'God's Messenger (peace be upon him) saw me wearing two garments dyed with safflower. He said to me: "These are of the type unbelievers wear. Do not wear them."' (Related by Muslim)
- Ibn 'Umar narrated from the Prophet (peace be upon him); he said: 'Do the opposite of the idolaters: grow your beards and trim your moustaches.' (Related by al-Bukhari and Muslim)
- Abu Hurayrah narrated: 'God's Messenger (peace be upon him) said: "Trim back your moustaches and let your beards

grow, doing the opposite of the Zoroastrians.'" (Related by Muslim)

- Ibn 'Abbās narrated: 'The Prophet liked to do the same as the people of earlier divine religions in what he had no special instructions. They used to let their hair down, while the idolaters used to part their hair. The Prophet dropped his hair over his forehead at first, and he parted his hair later.' (Related by al-Bukhari and Muslim)

The purpose of these instructions is clear in the very text of these hadiths. It is to give a distinctive character to Muslim men and women. An important result of such distinctive features is to avoid what apparent similarity may lead to of 'borrowing' some deviant ideas or imitating some unacceptable practices of other communities.

What we said about women emulating men is also applicable in the present context. To guard against emulating idolater or unbeliever women does not mean refraining from wearing a piece of clothing or adornment which is similar to what unbelievers wear. The focus is on the general appearance. What is important is that when a Muslim woman is seen, she is distinguished from non-Muslim women. We believe that when Muslim women implement the Islamic conditions in their attire, including the head covering, they will be distinguished from unbelievers. It is also important not to have any article that is symbolic to unbelievers. Such articles, even if very small, are disallowed.